15 Days of Prayer
With Don Bosco

Also in the *15 Days of Prayer* collection:

Saint Teresa of Ávila
The Curé of Ars
Pierre Teilhard de Chardin
Saint Bernard
Saint Augustine
Meister Eckhart
Thomas Merton
Saint Benedict
Charles de Foucauld
Saint Francis de Sales
Johannes Tauler
Saint Louis de Montfort
Saint Dominic
Saint Alphonsus Liguori
Saint John of the Cross
Saint Thérèse of Lisieux
Saint Catherine of Siena
Saint Bernadette of Lourdes
Saint Thomas Aquinas

15 DAYS OF PRAYER

WITH

Don Bosco

ROBERT SCHIÉLE

Translated by Victoria Hébert and Denis Sabourin

Liguori
LIGUORI, MISSOURI

Published by Liguori Publications
Liguori, Missouri
www.liguori.org
www.catholicbooksonline.com

This book is a translation of *Prier 15 Jours Avec Don Bosco*, published by Nouvelle Cité, 1991, Montrouge, France.

English Translation Copyright 2001 by Liguori Publications.

Library of Congress Cataloging-in-Publication Data

Schiéle, Robert.
    [Prier 15 jours avec Don Bosco. English]
    15 days of prayer with Don Bosco / Robert Schiéle ; [translated by] Victoria Hébert and Denis Sabourin. — 1st English ed.
        p. cm.
    Includes bibliographical references.
    ISBN 0-7648-0712-9 (pbk.)
    1. Bosco, Giovanni, Saint, 1815–1888—Meditations. 2. Spiritual life—Catholic Church. I. Title: Fifteen days of prayer with Don Bosco. II. Title.

BX4700.B75 S3813 2001
269'.6—dc21   2001018798

Printed in the United States of America
05 04 03 02 01   5 4 3 2 1
First English Edition 2001

Table of Contents

How to Use This Book

AN OLD CHINESE PROVERB, or at least what I am able to recall of what is supposed to be an old Chinese proverb, goes something like this: "Even a journey of a thousand miles begins with a single step." When you think about it, the truth of the proverb is obvious. It is impossible to begin any project, let alone a journey, without taking the first step. I think it might also be true, although I cannot recall if another Chinese proverb says it, "that the first step is often the hardest." Or, as someone else once observed, "the distance between a thought and the corresponding action needed to implement the idea takes the most energy." I don't know who shared that perception with me but I am certain it was not an old Chinese master!

With this ancient proverbial wisdom, and the not-so-ancient wisdom of an unknown contemporary sage still fresh, we move from proverbs to presumptions. How do these relate to the task before us?

I am presuming that if you are reading this introduction it is because you are contemplating a journey. My presumption is that you are preparing for a spiritual journey and that you have taken at least some of the first steps necessary to prepare for this journey. I also presume, and please excuse me if I am making too many presumptions, that in your preparation for the spiritual journey you have determined that you need a guide. From deep within the recesses of your deepest self, there was something that called you to consider Saint John Bosco as a potential companion. If my presumptions are correct, may I congratulate you on this decision? I think you have made a wise choice, a choice that can be confirmed by yet another source of wisdom, the wisdom that comes from practical experience.

Even an informal poll of experienced travelers will reveal a common opinion; it is very difficult to travel alone. Some might observe that it is even foolish. Still others may be even stronger in their opinion and go so far as to insist that it is necessary to have a guide, especially when you are traveling into uncharted waters and into territory that you have not yet experienced. I am of the personal opinion that a traveling companion is welcome under all circumstances. The thought of traveling alone, to some exciting destination without someone to share the journey with does not capture my imagination or channel my enthusiasm. However, with that being noted, what is simply a matter of preference on the normal journey becomes a matter of necessity when a person embarks on a spiritual journey.

The spiritual journey, which can be the most challenging of all journeys, is experienced best with a guide, a companion, or at the very least, a friend in whom you have placed your trust. This observation is not a preference or an opinion but rather an established spiritual necessity. All of the great saints with whom I am familiar had a spiritual director or a confessor who journeyed with them. Admittedly, at times the saint might well have traveled far beyond the experience of their guide and companion but more often than not they would return to their director and reflect on their experience. Understood in this sense, the director and companion provided a valuable contribution and necessary resource.

When I was learning how to pray (a necessity for anyone who desires to be a full-time and public "religious person"), the community of men that I belong to gave me a great gift.

Between my second and third year in college, I was given a one-year sabbatical, with all expenses paid and all of my personal needs met. This period of time was called novitiate. I was officially designated as a novice, a beginner in the spiritual journey, and I was assigned a "master," a person who was willing to lead me. In addition to the master, I was provided with every imaginable book and any other resource that I could possibly need. Even with all that I was provided, I did not learn how to pray because of the books and the unlimited resources, rather it was the master, the companion who was the key to the experience.

One day, after about three months of reading, of quiet and solitude, and of practicing all of the methods and descriptions of prayer that were available to me, the master called. "Put away the books, forget the method, and just listen." We went into a room, became quiet, and tried to recall the presence of God, and then, the master simply prayed out loud and permitted me to listen to his prayer. As he prayed, he revealed his hopes, his dreams, his struggles, his successes, and most of all, his relationship with God. I discovered as I listened that his prayer was deeply intimate but most of all it was self-revealing. As I learned about him, I was led through his life experience to the place where God dwells. At that moment I was able to understand a little bit about what I was supposed to do if I really wanted to pray.

The dynamic of what happened when the master called, invited me to listen, and then revealed his innermost self to me as he communicated with God in prayer, was important. It wasn't so much that the master was trying to reveal to me what needed to be said; he was not inviting me to pray with the same words that he used, but rather that he was trying to bring me to that place within myself where prayer becomes possible. That place, a place of intimacy and of self-awareness, was a necessary stop on the journey and it was a place that I needed to be led to. I could not have easily discovered it on my own.

The purpose of the volume that you hold in your hand is to lead you, over a period of fifteen days or, maybe more realistically, fifteen prayer periods, to a place where prayer is possible. If you already have a regular experience and practice of prayer, perhaps this volume can help lead you to a deeper place, a more intimate relationship with the Lord.

It is important to note that the purpose of this book is not to lead you to a better relationship with Saint John Bosco, your spiritual companion. Although your companion will invite you to share some of their deepest and most intimate thoughts, your companion is doing so only to bring you to that place where God dwells. After all, the true measurement of a companion for the journey is that they bring you to the place where you need to be, and then they step back, out of the picture. A guide who brings you to the desired destination and then sticks around is a very unwelcome guest!

Many times I have found myself attracted to a particular idea or method for accomplishing a task, only to discover that what seemed to be inviting and helpful possessed too many details. All of my energy went to the mastery of the details and I soon lost my enthusiasm. In each instance, the book that seemed so promising ended up on my bookshelf, gathering dust. I can assure you, it is not our intention that this book end up in your bookcase, filled with promise, but unable to deliver.

There are three simple rules that need to be followed in order to use this book with a measure of satisfaction.

Place: It is important that you choose a place for reading that provides the necessary atmosphere for reflection and that does not allow for too many distractions. Whatever place you choose needs to be comfortable, have the necessary lighting, and, finally, have a sense of "welcoming" about it. You need to be able to look forward to the experience of the journey. Don't travel steerage if you know you will be more comfortable in first class and if the choice is realistic for you. On the other hand, if first class is a distraction and you feel more comfortable and more yourself in steerage, then it is in steerage that you belong.

My favorite place is an overstuffed and comfortable chair in my bedroom. There is a light over my shoulder, and the chair reclines if I feel a need to recline. Once in a while, I get lucky and the sun comes through my window and bathes the entire room in light. I have other options and other places that are available to me but this is the place that I prefer.

Time: Choose a time during the day when you are most alert and when you are most receptive to reflection, meditation, and prayer. The time that you choose is an essential component. If you are a morning person, for example, you should choose a time that is in the morning. If you are more alert in the afternoon, choose an afternoon time slot; and if evening is your preference, then by all means choose the evening. Try to avoid "peak" periods in your daily routine when you know that you might be disturbed. The time that you choose needs to be your time and needs to work for you.

It is also important that you choose how much time you will spend with your companion each day. For some it will be possible to set aside enough time in order to read and reflect on all the material that is offered for a given day. For others, it might not be possible to devote one time to the suggested material for the day, so the prayer period may need to be extended for two, three, or even more sessions. It is not important how long it takes you; it is only important that it works for you and that you remain committed to that which is possible.

For myself I have found that fifteen minutes in the early morning, while I am still in my robe and pajamas and before my morning coffee, and even before I prepare myself for the day, is the best time. No one expects to see me or to interact with me because I have not yet "announced" the fact that I am awake or even on the move. However, once someone hears me in the bathroom, then my window of opportunity is gone. It is therefore important to me that I use the time that I have identified when it is available to me.

Freedom: It may seem strange to suggest that freedom is the third necessary ingredient, but I have discovered that it is most important. By freedom I understand a certain "stance toward life," a "permission to be myself and to be gentle and understanding of who I am." I am constantly amazed at how the human person so easily sets himself or herself up for disappointment and perceived failure. We so easily make judgments about ourselves and our actions and our choices, and very often those judgments are negative, and not at all helpful.

For instance, what does it really matter if I have chosen a place and a time, and I have missed both the place and the time for three days in a row? What does it matter if I have chosen, in that twilight time before I am completely awake and still a little sleepy, to roll over and to sleep for fifteen minutes more? Does it mean that I am not serious about the journey, that I really don't want to pray, that I am just fooling myself when I say that my prayer time is important to me? Perhaps, but I prefer to believe that it simply means that I am tired and I just wanted a little more sleep. It doesn't mean anything more than that. However, if I make it mean more than that, then I can become discouraged, frustrated, and put myself into a state where I might more easily give up. "What's the use? I might as well forget all about it."

The same sense of freedom applies to the reading and the praying of this text. If I do not find the introduction to each day helpful, I don't need to read it. If I find the questions for reflection at the end of the appointed day repetitive, then I should choose to close the book and go my own way. Even if I discover that the reflection offered for the day is not the one that I prefer and that the one for the next day seems more inviting, then by all means, go on to the one for the next day.

That's it! If you apply these simple rules to your journey you should receive the maximum benefit and you will soon find yourself at your destination. But be prepared to be surprised. If you have never been on a spiritual journey you should know that the "travel brochures" and the other descriptions that you might have heard are nothing compared to the real thing. There is so much more than you can imagine.

A final prayer of blessing suggests itself:

> Lord, catch me off guard today.
> Surprise me with some moment of beauty
>   or pain
> So that at least for the moment
> I may be startled into seeing that you are
>   here in all your splendor,
> Always and everywhere,
> Barely hidden,
> Beneath,
> Beyond,
> Within this life I breathe.

Frederick Buechner

REV. THOMAS M. SANTA, CSsR
LIGUORI, MISSOURI
FEAST OF THE PRESENTATION, 1999

Introduction and Brief Chronology of the Life of Saint John Bosco

JOHN BOSCO, 1815–1888

Soon after the Napoleonic Wars, Giovanni Melchior Bosco was born to a poor family in Belchi, a hillside hamlet near Castelnuovo, Piedmont, (not far from Turin) Italy, on August 16, 1815. His father, Francis, a farmer, died of pneumonia when John was only two; and his mother, Margaret Occhiena, was left to care for the family of four as well as her chronically ill mother-in-law.

At the age of nine, John had a prophetic dream that would affect the rest of his life. In this first of many future dreams, John saw wild beasts turned into gentle lambs and unruly children becoming well behaved. This showed him what he should pursue in life—he was convinced that he should work as a priest and teacher. His first formal schooling, at the age of fourteen, came from his parish priest. John had worked long and hard to be able to attend school and paid for his subsequent education as well as room and board, himself, in Castelnuovo. At the age of twenty, he entered the seminary in Chieri and, after six intensive years of study, was ordained a priest on the eve of Trinity Sunday (June 5) by the archbishop of Turin. From that time on, he was known as Don Bosco.

Upon leaving the seminary, Don Bosco went to Turin where he accompanied Don Joseph Cafasso (later to be canonized himself) on his prison visits. There, he saw deplorable conditions and even children, living there, awaiting the fate of the gallows. He vowed to devote his life to rescue these unfortunate souls. On the feast of the Immaculate Conception, December 8, 1841, Don Bosco, while he was dressing for Mass, heard a commotion in the sacristy as the sacristan was refusing entrance to a sixteen-year-old street urchin, Bartolomeo Garelli. Don Bosco called the boy back and here began the foundation of his "oratories," named probably after those of Saint Philip Neri, and because prayer was also their main focus. He placed these under the patronage of Saint Francis de Sales. Don Bosco began his ministry to the youth by the formation of catechism classes which would meet after Sunday Mass. In these meetings, he would offer Mass, free schooling, catechism, lunch, music, recreation, and Vespers: he soon had a following of over four hundred! As the numbers increased, Don Bosco had the problem of a suitable meeting place. When they had fine weather, they strolled in the countryside around Turin, but when the winds and rains blew, this posed a problem.

In 1844, Don Bosco was appointed chaplain in the *Rifugio* (orphanage) and was able to secure two rooms on the grounds, which he converted into a chapel and a place to be used for his oratories. Relieved of this post, he was able to devote his entire time to the oratories. At this time, he also began his night school where technical skills were taught. After overcoming many problems, displacements, obstacles, accusations, and difficulties, Don Bosco was able to purchase a house, where he founded the Oratory of Saint Francis de Sales (his first Salesian home). This became a multipurpose building: a hostel, a training center, and a school—no one had to leave to get either their technical training or their formal education. A church was built, the buildings enlarged, and eventually the great basilica, dedicated to Our Lady, Help of Christians, rose up at this site (it was consecrated on June 9, 1868). Don Bosco's own mother, "Mama Margaret" as she came to be known, devoted the last ten years of her life to these first Salesians.

The Salesian congregation was founded in the same year as the church was built, with the fifty priests and teachers who had been helping him. They formed a society under a common rule which was approved, provisionally in 1869, and finally in 1874, by Pope Pius IX. Later, in 1872, along with Saint Maria Mazzarello, a congregation of nuns would also be founded to do similar work for girls (Daughters of Our Lady, Help of Christians). A third order, the Union of Cooperator Salesians was founded as well (1874).

In 1875, the Salesians first expanded their territory, reaching out to France and South America. (They would later go to most of the European and South American countries as well as the United States.)

At the time of his death, on January 31, 1888, Don Bosco could count 774 religious brothers and priests and 313 religious sisters spread across 250 institutions and houses, from which 18,000 apprentices graduated annually. Don Bosco was canonized by Pope Pius XI on Easter Sunday, 1934. In January 1989, Pope John Paul II proclaimed him the "Father and Master of all youth."

Don Bosco was a man who loved the youth in society and devoted his life to their education and training. He loved these youngsters, but also respected them; this is what drew them to him. He was a man with a mission, there was always one duty more urgent than the next, but he never appeared to be hurried or impatient. It was said that he was always smiling, ready to help, hear a confession, or go to see a sick person. He never slept more than five hours a night, often much less. He had great faith in Providence—this was the secret of his calm approach. It is said that the many miracles that were attributed to him were due, in large part, to his trust in Providence.

Let us not forget that he was also a very human person— he was plagued with varicose veins, eczema, and increasing blindness. With reference to his death, it was said that he died of exhaustion, seeking funding for his programs. His body rests in his great basilica alongside those of his collaborator, Saint Maria Mazzarello and his pupil, Saint Dominic Savio.

THE HOLY SPIRIT OF GOD SENT HIM

Don Bosco was a gift from the Holy Spirit to the Church. The Holy Spirit sent him to proclaim the Good News to the poor, the marginalized, and the most destitute to bring them happiness. His training bore the mark of a master, Alphonsus Liguori, who revealed to him a close and tender God, as well as the vocation of a Christian—a pilgrim on a long journey. Saint Francis de Sales, whom he choose as the patron for his work, conveyed his tenderness and smiling goodness to him. His goal was to bring happiness to the world, the kind that freed and built mankind up. His writings show this to us, especially the two which provide the material for the meditations in this book: *The Educated Young Man*, a devotional book that was published shortly after his ordination (which was edited and re-edited a number of times until his death); and *The Month of Mary* (1858), which includes thirty short, practical, and lively chapters centered on Jesus Christ the Savior and witness of the Father. For him, the path of life was a stroll towards happiness in familiarity with God.

For these fifteen days in his company, the itinerary is the

same. Jesus Christ is the center of all communication. He is "the way, the truth, and the life," the source of our happiness. In his own way, Don Bosco proclaims the beatitudes (day one). Jesus reveals his Father, the amazing creator, through his works and his gifts; and he saves us from evil (day two). Jesus joins us: he is our companion, our friend, and our guide (day three). Jesus founded the Church, the most holy and fruitful Mother; Don Bosco is her loving son and dauntless servant (day four). Mary, the shepherdess of his initial dream, is immaculate and beautiful, the helper and the lady with the protective mantle (day five). Jesus made himself become man so that we will become saints following his lead. Don Bosco opens a living path of holiness; he conceived it as a response to radical love, to be assumed amidst the dullness of daily life (day six). But its monotone duration is impregnated with happiness that traces its source to God's heart (day seven). Jesus worked with his hands in Nazareth; Don Bosco, all throughout his life, spoke repeatedly of the necessary benefit of work (day eight). Jesus gathered crowds together; Don Bosco, a born gatherer, reminds us that the path of life is made easier through the closeness of the disciples who are driven by the same faith (day nine). The God of the Christians is a fire that devours, spreading to all four corners of the world; Saint John Bosco said: "Lord, give me the souls and take the rest!" He made the poor people become his privileged friends (day ten). Jesus took up his cross and invited all to follow; Don Bosco repeatedly said: "There are no roses without thorns; if we suffer with Jesus Christ on earth, we will reign with him in heaven" (day eleven). Like Abraham, we will walk on earth in the presence of God through prayer (day twelve). Finally, on this path, certain provisions will restore our strength: divine forgiveness, the spring of the heart (day thirteen), and the bread of life, the manna of resurrection (day fourteen). The pilgrimage ends in the house of our Father in heaven. Don Bosco invites us there: let us go, in song, to the house of the Lord (day fifteen).

That is the message that I want to give to you. Right from my childhood, I have been captivated by Don Bosco. I got to know him through my Salesian teachers, and my master of novices, who had the opportunity to meet him at the end of his life. They had seen his penetrating gaze, responded to his smile, had either received sacramental forgiveness from him or heard him speak which, for one or another of them, had shaken up their life. They had remembered his famous words: "Remain happy! Let nothing bother you! Save your soul! I love you because you are young!" These words of yesterday will echo for us again today.

In this book, we will let Don Bosco speak directly to us, quite convincingly, as if he was speaking at the beginning of the twenty-first century. All of the remarks that we will borrow from him have not come directly from his mouth or his pen, far from it! But a profound and extensive knowledge of his thinking and his speech allows me to make him speak, I hope, and not betray him too much. Thus we will hear him each day through a text that he has left for us. At times, he will use dialogue, a mode of communication with which he was very familiar. At all times, the tone will be kept simple and direct; we will often make reference to the Bible.

Don Bosco returns! Just as the youth of the world sang on the occasion of the centennial of his death (1988): "Don Bosco, today, your signature is a smile!" May the Holy Spirit make us messengers of this happiness in order to bring fruit to the places where God has planted us!

15 Days of Prayer
With Don Bosco

DAY ONE

Take Your Road of Happiness

Life is a journey, a journey to God, a journey with God. If we seek to be with God in our life's journey, then we journey with happiness to Happiness. In each of our lives, God calls us outside of ourselves, calls us to serve the Church, proclaim the Gospel, nourish ourselves with the Word, watch over our health, seek the comfort of Mary, help those in need, and to know the love of God and walk in his presence. By seeking to do the will of God in our lives, we will be happy both now and in eternity.

Friend, consider that God created you in his image, that he gave you a body and an immortal soul. Furthermore, through baptism, he made you his child. He has loved you forever and still loves you like a tender Father. He created you only to love

I

*him, serve him in this world, and, in this way, to merit, one
day, to be happy with him in heaven. Thus, you are not here on
earth to have fun, earn money, eat, or to sleep. God gave his
own life to you for a marvelous destiny. He created you to love
him, serve him, and to save your soul in happiness!*

*The devil has two traps to divert the youth away from true
happiness. The first is to make them believe that serving the
Lord will make them sad people, without leisure, people who
aren't in the loop! But that isn't true, my friends. The other
trap is to make you believe that the youth have a good amount
of time to think about serious things. Be careful, my friends,
even if you have many chances to get old, you must, today, at
all cost, make a success of your youth. It takes up your whole
life, both in this lifetime and the next!* (John Bosco, The Educated Young Man, *Turin, 1847, Introduction*).

LIFE IS A ROAD

My friends, I didn't discover the direction of the Christian road
and the secret of happiness in scholarly books, but through
contact with the distress of the young people, at the beginning
of my ministry in Turin. These idle children, excluded and en-
gaged in dead-end activities, were seeking a guide and a friend.
I decided to become that friend and their traveling companion.
What is the Christian road?

First, it is a voyage. One walk has remained unforgettable
for me: the forty miles that led my mother and I from our hamlet to the big city to install the first nest for our "fledglings."
The date was November 3, 1846. An adventure began for us!

Saint Alphonsus Liguori told us: "Life is a voyage towards
eternity." It is a voyage with its connections, stops and starts,
and uncertainties. It follows the stages of life, accompanies our

history, unites our friends and our relatives. It is a route that leads us to the shores of our salvation. Recalling the image of Saint Francis de Sales, "We must live in the boat where we are for the course of this life and stay there willingly and lovingly" (Letter of April 7, 1617).

THE ROAD IS A PILGRIMAGE

It was my joy to have made numerous pilgrimages and to accompany many young people during our celebrated autumn walks. A pilgrimage is the path of a believer who sets a goal and commits himself to it. He is not hindered by baggage; he follows his route with the heart of a poor person, in faith. He wants to meet God. His exodus is a confident walk to a promised land or to "...the city that has sure foundations, whose architect and builder is God" (Heb 11:10).

THE ROAD IS A RACECOURSE

When I was in college, I challenged a professional runner who crossed the city in two and a half minutes, the speed of a train full out! I beat him and there was a great celebration with my friends. Life is also a race, but it is sown with thorns! It is the racecourse of a soldier where he must fight to win, as "a good soldier for Jesus Christ," and bring back the crown that doesn't fade, "the crown of righteousness" (2 Tim 4:8). To the young people, I often described, in detail, the armature of the true soldier of God and prepared them to fight for the Christian life. Life is a road, a road that makes people strong.

A ROAD OF HAPPINESS

I loved these words from Scripture: "Train children in the right way, and when old, they will not stray" (Prov 22:6). And I proposed a road of happiness.

I again see my comings and goings under the archways of Turin, to the places bristling with young people. I mingled in their games, I listened to their questions; we would go and have "a pint," we would discuss the meaning of life and I reminded them: "Friends, happiness can't be found in games, money, drink, or women." There were also many houses of ill repute in my neighborhood in Valdocco. They were only for quick pleasure; they sold a mirage of happiness. Happiness is made to last. When you go to a play or a concert, don't you ask for an "encore" or two at the end to make it last longer?

Then, what is happiness? It is born from a desire of the heart and the choice of God. Do you know this profound remark that Saint Augustine made: "Happiness is the possession that is both pleasant and intense for all that we could desire"? It isn't found in the rose that will fade, it dwells in a heart that loves and hopes. It is won like a battle, like the conquest of steep summits, climbed by a true athlete for God, alone or together, as a team.

Happiness flows, then, like a pure source of water. It inaugurates a new world, the kingdom, the world of Jesus. The beatitudes are the keys to this kingdom.

I offered them to the boys and girls of my era. On each page of my book, *The Educated Young Man*, I repeated "Beati voi": Happiness is yours. Today, I proclaim it, by catching your eyes, my friends, both young and not so young: "Happiness is yours." Welcome the words of the beatitudes.

THE BEATITUDES FOR A ROAD

Happy is the one who knows that he is tenderly loved by God who is the Father and Savior in Jesus Christ! He made his life into an "I love you" and walked with assurance under the gaze of God which was enough for his happiness.

Happy is the one who discovers that God is the God of

happiness, a happiness that gives! He makes himself the sower through his smile, humor, and the peace in his heart. He proclaimed: "For the Lord God is a sun and a shield" (Ps 84:11).

Happy is the one who watches over his health, making sure that he wisely balances work and rest, food and sleep! He will be strong and healthy, "...like the trees planted by streams of water, which yield their fruit in its season..." (Ps 1:3).

Happy is the one who knows that, with Jesus, "more is in him" and that holiness makes his baptism blossom! It will be contagious and his happiness "will awake the dawn" (Ps 57:8).

Happy is the one who helps an excluded youngster back to his feet, one who had been broken by failure and despair. His name will "be written" like a star in the heavens.

Happy is the one who walks in the presence of God, and, with the heart of a child, joins the One who is "standing at the door, knocking" (Rev 3:20). His gaze will be transformed by the light and he will say: "I have made the Lord God my refuge" (Ps 73:28).

Happy is the one who nourishes himself with the bread of the Word, of the Eucharist, and forgiveness! It will be "the good bread" for the brothers and the source of holiness.

Happy is the one who places his hands, every day, in those of Mary! In her, he will find the source of all beauty and all peace.

Happy is the one who takes his share of suffering to proclaim the Gospel (see 2 Tim 1:8)! For "I can do all things through him who strengthens me" (Phil 4:13) and will share, in the Easter of heaven, the happiness of God's friends.

Happy is the servant of the Church, this most holy mother, who gave us life and teaches us God's alphabet! He will have the heart of an apostle, a witness to "our God who is a consuming fire" (Heb 12:29).

Happy are you, friend, if you take this path of happiness

today! Happiness will sing in your heart for "the kingdom of God is among you" (Lk 17:21). One day, it will explode in the eternal spring of paradise.

GOD MAKES OUR WAY

The believer knows that he is accompanied and was preceded by God.

GOD LED ISRAEL

He traveled along with the children of Israel. "The Lord your God…goes before you on the way" (Deut 1:32–33). And there is a sign—the cloud, the presence of the faithful God "…preserving the way of his faithful ones" (Prov 2:8).

GOD REVEALS HIMSELF TO JESUS

In Bethlehem, Jesus made the All-Powerful One visible. His star guided the wise men, his Word revealed the presence of the Father: "Whoever has seen me, has seen the Father." He proclaims himself as the living road: "I am the truth, the way, and the life." He said: "Come to me, become my disciples!" and "I am with you always, to the end of the age" (Mt 28:20). The first Christians called the path of the risen One, the "Way" (Acts 22:4), the young Church born on the day of the Pentecost. Jesus is the sole road to their happiness.

GOD ACCOMPANIES OUR HISTORY

By writing down my memories for my dear sons, at the request of Pope Pius IX, I made this acknowledgment: "God himself made everything happen in its own time." God created our history. I read his signature in the important events where he revealed his presence: the dream I had at the age of nine, our installation at the Pinardi house on Easter, 1846, the approval of our Rules on April 3, 1874. I recognized him in meetings: those with Garelli and the first orphans we welcomed; those with Comollo, the unequaled friend of the college and the seminary; those with Savio, the boy who was crazy for God, that apostle with the heart of fire; and even in my faithful companion "Grigio," the providential dog who saved my life more than once. I discovered him in trials: in the brutal death of Don Calosso, my venerable master, and in the departure for heaven of my holy mother Margaret. I discovered him on the occasion of my first Communion, my confirmation at the age of eighteen, my ordination, and at my first Mass in the village where I was born. Let us not forget the departure of the first missionaries for Argentina, when our religious family crossed the oceans. That was on November 11, 1875.

God, himself, made everything happen in its own time, with Mary the faithful mother who accompanied him, step for step, in our history.

Friends, the road is yours. Leave to seek true happiness. Even today, Saint Augustine's call has retained all of its freshness and strength: "Walk and sing! Sing and Walk!" Happiness is waiting for you!

REFLECTION QUESTIONS

How do I respond to God's call to move outside of myself in my life? When I do respond to this call, why is it that I feel so refreshed and fulfilled? In what ways do I serve the Church, proclaim the Gospel, nourish myself with the Word, watch over my health, seek the comfort of Mary, help those in need, and know the love of God and walk in his presence? What emotions am I feeling, what expectations do I have, as I begin these fifteen days of prayer with Don Bosco?

God Is Our Very Good Father

FOCUS POINT

The Father loves us so much that he sent us his only son. The Father is reunited with his creation by the Incarnation, passion, death, and Resurrection of Jesus Christ. As creatures of God, we sometimes forget our place—abandon our humility—believing that we are more than we actually are. We sometimes believe that we do not need God and his grace in our lives. But it is the goodness and love of God that sustains us and gives our life meaning. Without God, we are empty, sad, and without hope. But with God, all things are possible.

When I say the dignity of a Christian, I mean the great dignity that you have acquired, when, through baptism, you had been received into the arms of our mother, the Church. Baptism opened the doors of the Church to you and delivered you from evil. At the very moment of your baptism, God gave his amazing love to you. In your heart, he deposited faith, hope, and charity. Having become a Christian, you can lift your eyes to heaven and cry: "The God of heaven and earth is also my Father. He is my Father, he loves me, he asks that I call him by this name: Our Father, who art in heaven."

Jesus the Savior calls me his brother and, as his brother, I belong to him. I share his merits, passion, death, glory, and dignity. He even wants to give me God as a Father, the Church as a mother, and the Word as a guide (John Bosco, The Month of Mary, *Turin, 1858, ninth day).*

"I CREATED THE WORLD FOR YOU"

I didn't know my father. My first memory is not the surprise of a toy or the tenderness of a kiss, but the words of my mother, sobbing, telling me, next to the bed of my father who had just died, "My little John, you no longer have a father!" I was twenty-one months old. This memory affected me for the rest of my life. When, in Turin, I welcomed Garelli and all of the other orphans, I understood their suffering. With them, I turned, like a big brother, to the Father in heaven who watches over us with tenderness, our creator. To pray to him today, we will use the format of a meditation dialogue between the Father in heaven and a Christian, his son.

Our Father: Lift your eyes, my son, and look at all that exists in heaven and on earth; the moon, the stars, the air, water, and fire. There was a time when all of these elements didn't exist. Through my all-powerfulness, I drew them from nothingness, I created them: it is for that reason that I am the creator. It was I who said, "Let there be light!" and it spread across the universe. It was I who denoted the limits of the earth, filled the oceans with fish, and made the green forests grow. By saying "Let it be done," the sun, moon, and stars lit the sky. And I saw that it was good.

The son: Father, how beautiful your works are! How grand they are!

Our Father: But creation was not finished. I created man. I wanted to establish him as the king of creation, a king filled with gifts. Plants live, grow, and multiply; animals understand, but do not speak. Only man is able to reason, express himself through speech, and love. I gave him a soul, a soul created in my image, a soul that thinks about and desires happiness, an immortal soul whose desire for eternity can only find its rest in me. And I saw that it was good.

The son: How many marvels there are in your gifts, Lord! But man isn't a solitary being. How is he connected to creation?

Our Father: My son, I created the universe for you, but I wanted to create it with you. In creation, man is not a spectator, but an actor. I made him my associate, my right arm, responsible for filling and dominating the earth. I made him a procreator. Do you understand, my son? In the body of man and woman, I etched the power to create life through a relationship of body and heart filled with mystery. This mystery is so great that no one can fully understand it. Man can transmit life and communicate my love. That is a great responsibility.

But I always remain close to you, my son. It is my voice that speaks to you from the depth of your heart. It is my hand that designed the arch of the rainbow in the sky. Discover my handiwork in the creation, my son, it speaks of me.

March in my presence like Abraham, my witness!

"YOU ARE MY BELOVED CHILD"

The son: Lord, how great this man is, the work of your hands! But, tell me, Father, how, as a simple creature, did I become your child?

Our Father: I took a long path to enter into the history of man, a path of steps. Love took the first steps....

I chose Israel for my people. Through Hosea, the prophet, I said, "It was I who taught him to walk and I took him up in my arms...I led him with cords of human kindness, with bands of love. I was to them like those who lift infants to their cheeks" (Hos 11:3–4). Then, I revealed myself in Jesus: when the time came, through the Holy Spirit, I begat my Son in the womb of Mary, the most pure. At Jesus' baptism, my voice arose: "This is my Son, the Beloved, with whom I am well pleased" (Mt 3:17). Jesus said, "My Father and I are one"—and he entrusted his friends with his prayer which is also yours: "Our Father, who art in heaven...." Finally, I called you into the Church. The Church was born from the pierced heart from which water and blood flowed, figures of baptism and the Eucharist to beget and nourish the children of God.

That is why, at your baptism, my son, you became "my beloved child." At that instant, I took possession of your heart; at that instant, I dwelled within you with the Holy Spirit who "makes all things new again"; at that instant, your soul, created in my image, took on my resemblance, the "features of my face." You then lifted your eyes to heaven, to me, your creator, and said this prayer: "I believe in you, my God! You love me, you are my Father. You gave me a name and I call you my Father."

The son: Baptism gave me a new life, but I am still a sinner. Why, my God, is there such evil in me, such hardship in the world?

"I DELIVER YOU FROM EVIL"

Our Father: By entrusting human beings with the keys of paradise, I offered happiness. I created man and woman, free and able to change the world and give life. They had everything necessary to be happy when the drama burst, the drama of freedom and man's choice.

There were three of them in the garden. In its image-laden language, the Bible explains: Adam, Eve, and the serpent. I had forbidden them from touching the fruit of the tree, but the serpent hissed his words of disobedience. Evil slipped into creation, and the couple hid themselves. The evil was the devil, the alluring serpent. The evil was the refusal of a freedom other than that of man: that of his creator, his benefactor. The evil was the innocence that was lost.

Hardship came to the world. Hardship was the suspicion and the doubts introduced to the couple, the wounds of the origins—the original sin—that would come to be transmitted from generation to generation. The sin was there, like the worm in the fruit. Man turned his back on the creator, his friend. He said: "I have the right to be free. I do what I want to do. My only master is myself."

In the midst of this mess, I wanted to make everything new again and I created a new world, a second creation, a new chance for humanity. Jesus, the true Adam, opened this new era where love finally triumphs. A new world was born in Jesus. I loved you, my son, and I proved my love by giving you my own Son to break your chains and free you from all sin. And I saw that all of this was good, my son!

The son: Glory to you, our Father in heaven! Glory to you, Jesus our Savior! Glory to you, Holy Spirit who renews our earth!

My friends, such is the holy history of the love and mercy of God our Father. Let us praise him together with this simple prayer:

Our Father in Heaven,
You who made us your beloved children,
Blessed are you for your beauty,
Blessed are you for your tenderness,
Blessed are you for your faithfulness,
Put the bread of the body into our hands
and into our hearts the bread of holiness.
Let us take the first step
to have peace each day.
Make us agents of unity
and not of separation
for a fraternal road.

Make us strong against the devil
who tempts us,
You, our rock,
You, our shield,
You, our sun!
For all time. Amen.

REFLECTION QUESTIONS

How does humility factor into my life? Do I sometimes forget
my place as a creature of God and try to do things on my own,
without calling on the grace of God in prayer? What steps can
I take to become a more humble servant of God? Might fasting
help me to center myself on the fact that without God, without
all that he provides, I am empty and wanting? Might I consult
a priest, a religious, or a spiritual director in my quest to incorporate greater humility into my spiritual life?

DAY THREE

Jesus Is Our
Friend and Guide

FOCUS POINT

We all encounter pain and suffering in our lives. This suffering can be quite discouraging to a life that is not centered in Jesus. When we live our lives in God, with Jesus Christ as our friend and guide, the suffering we experience has already been known by him. Thus, he shares our pain; and just as our Lord emerged from his pain and suffering in the Resurrection, so we will be brought closer to God by the pain and suffering we know in our own lives. Every corner of our lives (including the darkness of suffering) must be given over to God.

All of our beloved Lord's actions are a series of gestures of his generous bounty. Never has he harshly rejected the greatest of sinners. What tender love he manifests towards those who have sinned against him. Peter denied him three times. He looked at him with compassion, he made him look into himself, and offered him a love that was completely new.

Oh, with what love, with what tenderness God embraces those who had once strayed but have now returned to him! Let us remember the parable of the Lost Sheep. The good shepherd found it, put it on his shoulders, carried it back to his house, and called to his friends: "Rejoice with me for I have found the lamb that I had lost." In the parable of the Prodigal Son, Jesus said: the Father, he is our God! It is this loving Father who perceived his son lost and ran to meet him, and, even before he had spoken, embraced him, covering him with kisses, almost fainting with tenderness—that is the greatness of the consolation he felt (John Bosco, Exercise of the Devotion to the Mercy of God, *Turin, 1846, fourth meditation*).

"COME AND SEE"

John and two of his disciples followed Jesus to find out where he lived. Jesus replied: "'Come and see.' They came and saw where he was staying, and they remained with him that day" (Jn 1:39).

Let us take the time to remain with Jesus for all of today. Let us look at him and listen to him silently. Two characteristics will nourish our contemplation: the good shepherd and the "pierced heart."

The actions of the good shepherd are numerous in the Gospel: to the sick, the errant crowds, the mourning widows, and all of the underprivileged. We remember the tenderness of the Lord towards the children and the young people. Here is Jesus as he arrives in a village of Galilee with his apostles. The urchins rush up to him. He greets them, smiles at them, hugs the smallest and looks upon their innocent faces. His words fall on a stupefied audience: "Their angels see the face of my Father"; "Whoever makes himself small will be great in the kingdom"; and "Whoever welcomes one of these children in my name, it is I who they are welcoming."

According to Jesus, childhood inaugurates a new world. Not only did he welcome the young people, he also healed the son of a Roman officer, he raised from the dead the son of a widow from Nain, looked upon the young rich man and loved him, and from a young boy he received seven loaves of bread and a few fish and fed four thousand people (see Mk 8).

Jesus loved the young people: "They are God's delights."

"The pierced heart" (see Jn 19:34) challenges us. *The Imitation of Christ* declares: "If you had entered into the heart of Jesus just once, you would know something of his ardent love." Jesus' heart tells us: "Come to me, all you that are weary and are carrying heavy burdens and I will give you rest" (Mt 11:28).

What tenderness, what humility, what gentleness! These gestures and words from Jesus inspired my attitude towards young people. His affectionate goodness has become a path of education for me. My educational method is founded in the heart of Jesus.

"BECOME MY DISCIPLE"

Jesus was clear. After having opened his heart to his disciples, he taught them. "Take my yoke upon you, and learn from me; for I am gentle and humble in heart, and you will find rest for your souls" (Mt 11:29). The master invites his friends to imitate him. To imitate is not to blindly copy a model, but to follow an example, that of a witness: he returns to what is invisible, awakens love, and commits to it. Jesus is the Father's witness.

In the portrait of a Christian, outlined in the book, *The Key to Paradise*, I explained it: "No one can belong to Jesus unless he imitates him. In the life and actions of a Christian, we must see the actions of Jesus Christ."

Like Jesus, let us love young people. Here is my declaration of love for young people in *The Educated Young Man*: "Young people, see how much the Lord loves you! The youth is the most precious sector of society. On you are founded all of our hopes for a happy future.... My friends, I love you with all my heart. It is enough that you are young for me to give you my affection. You will find people who are holier and wiser than I am, but will not so easily find a friend who loves you like I do, in Jesus Christ, and who wants your happiness."

Just as Jesus kept his word, let us be faithful to our commitments as "good soldiers of Christ Jesus" (2 Tim 2:3). On Pentecost, 1867, I addressed this letter to my beloved children in Turin: "Whoever wants to be my disciple must follow me through prayer and penance and deny himself, Jesus said. If he assumes the cross of daily difficulties and follows me, just how far will he go? All the way to death and, if necessary, all the way to death on the cross. In our society, that is what is accomplished by the person who uses his strengths in his mission as a priest, in teaching, all the way to a death, even a violent one, in prison, in exile, by the sword, water, or fire. Having endured suffering or death with Jesus Christ on earth, he will go and rejoice with him in heaven!" It is through the cross that we will reach glory.

Like Jesus, let us be strong in our suffering. I sent this little note to a missionary in Argentina: "Work, but work for the love of Jesus; suffer everything rather than sacrifice charity." A few days before his death, Dominic Savio said to the doctor who prescribed bleedings to soothe his illness: "It's a little thing, a few pricks, compared to the nails hammered into the hands of our innocent Savior!" In primary school, Dominic had been falsely accused of something by his classmates. Truth had won out. He declared to the teacher: "I thought about our divine Savior who had been unjustly slandered." To imitate Jesus Christ through the trials of the apostles is to suffer with and for him.

Through Jesus, we will receive our reward. The true Christian will say, with Paul: "It is not I who lives, but Jesus who lives in me." He will receive the reward and be glorified with Jesus. We always end up being changed by the one that we love. The imitation of Jesus Christ becomes a transformation. It only happens through a vision of paradise.

"I WILL GO WITH YOU"

On the road to Emmaus, Jesus came to join his friends. He comes again onto our roads. He goes ahead of us, he accompanies us, he walks with us.

I reminded Madeleine Martini who, at the age of twenty-four, left her rich family for the novitiate of The Daughters of Our Lady, Help of Christians, of the following: "(1) we don't go to glory without great fatigue; (2) we are not alone, Jesus is with us and Saint Paul said that with the help of Jesus we can do everything in the One who gives us strength; (3) the person who abandons their home, parents, and friends in order to follow the divine master, assures himself of a treasure in heaven that no one can take away from him; (4) the great reward that is prepared in heaven should encourage and support any worry on earth. Have courage, Jesus is with us. When you have thorns, put them with those on Jesus Christ's crown."

Jesus walks with us to lead us to the eternal light. Listen to the last words of Dominic Savio: "Whoever has Jesus for a friend does not fear death." Six year later, François Besucco, while looking at me from his sickbed, his eyes full of light, said: "Jesus is my friend and my companion, I have nothing to fear. Have I not everything to hope for through his great mercy?"

Jesus walks with us.

My friends, each day I leaned on him. Each day, he has been my friend and my guide. May he be your strength and your happiness. We can do everything in the One who makes us strong. The words of Saint Paul are a song of hope: "Remember Jesus Christ, raised from the dead...if we have died with him, we will also live with him...we will also reign with him" (2 Tim 2:8, 11–12).

REFLECTION QUESTIONS

How do I perceive pain and suffering when I am visited by them in my own life? Do I feel abandoned by God at these times, or do I see these periods of pain and suffering as opportunities to grow closer to God by sharing in the pain that Jesus Christ suffered for love of us? When I am in the midst of suffering, it is very easy (and sometimes important) to focus only on myself. Am I still able to get outside myself during these times of suffering, and share the love and generosity of God with those around me?

DAY FOUR

The Church Is Your Family

FOCUS POINT

We are members of the Body of Christ, the people of God, the Church. We are united by the Head of the Church, Jesus Christ. The other members of the Church support us when we fall, welcoming us back into the fold when the Good Shepherd calls us to return from our straying. The Church nourishes us by its sacramental nature; we encounter God in the sacraments, and we are brought to greater depth in our relationship with him. We are called to be active and vocal members of the Church, responding to those within and without the Church in a spirit of love and imitation of Christ.

The Church is similar to a mother who is filled with tenderness and affection, and who wants to receive, always and every-

where, all of those who want to enter into her maternal womb. This Church must always be visible to everyone. That is why the Gospel compares it to a column against which all of the enemies of our soul are broken, and to a rock upon which leans the great building, which must last forever, and to a kingdom, a city, a family.... The Church is called universal because it welcomes everyone and possesses all of the doctrine taught by Jesus Christ and preached by the apostles. It is called holy for its founder is the source of all holiness. It is called apostolic for its pastors are the successors of the apostles (John Bosco, The Month of Mary, *Turin, 1858, fourth day).*

I BELIEVE IN ONE CHURCH

With a filial heart, I would like to again state, today, my faith in this one Church, holy and apostolic, which is the ark of salvation for me.

There is one Church, for it only forms one family. In the Scriptures, this family is compared to a kingdom, a city, a citadel; we are the subjects, the citizens, the defenders, the members. Do you know what the inscription is on the baptistery of Saint John Lateran Church in Rome? There we read: "At this source, the Church, our mother, gave birth, from her virginal womb, to the son who was conceived by the breath of God." Do we not recognize, in these words, the place and the act of our new birth? Is the Church not the womb where the complete unity of the body occurs? One sole faith, one sole baptism, one sole Church. Saint Cyprian and Saint Augustine explained forcefully: "The one who doesn't have the Church for a mother cannot have God for their Father." There is one Church because its visible Head is Christ, the living Person of the Holy Trinity; there is only one, for it was founded on Peter, the "rock," and, according to Tradition, I can say; "Where Peter is, there you will find the Church."

There is one Church with one pope who is the Vicar of Christ. I met two popes, Pius IX and Leo XIII. I entrusted my projects to them and asked for their help for the foundation of my two religious families and my third order. I begged for their blessing for my young people and my missionaries. I always wanted my disciples to be their devoted sons. On the occasion of his episcopal jubilee, I wrote the following to Pius IX: "Most Holy Father, our work is your work. All of the Salesians are yours. They are ready to work where it would please you. They would be happy to give their goods through love for this God of whom you are the vicar on earth. Bless your sons and may this benediction make them strong in battle, courageous in sufferings, constant in work so that they may, one day, gather around you to sing and eternally bless the mercies of the Lord." One sole pastor, one sole fold, one sole family.

I BELIEVE IN THE HOLY CHURCH

The Church is holy for only God is holy. He is "the source of all holiness," which he communicates to his children through the sacraments and the Word, "for we are the shoots of the true vine." The Church is holy but it is not a Church of saints. I had been a witness to the blindness and the harshness of priests when faced with the distress of the youth and the poor who begged, at their doors, for food, for truth, and for justice. I experienced criticism and slander from a clergyman regarding my initiatives and my foundations for the youth. I have lived the Church's exclusions of non-Christians, notably Jews. However, with these people, I found active cooperators and I came to welcome some of their children into our works.

I confronted sects; it was a rude awakening. One day, during a catechism class, a bullet that was shot through the window passed through my clothing between my left arm and my breast to finally lodge itself in the wall. A price had been put on my head!

I was also confronted by holy people, authentic men of God—even my archbishop, Monsignor Lorenzo Gastaldi. Our temperaments and methods were quite different. He trained a zealous and fervent clergy according to the principles of the Council of Trent; I was preparing active religious, dedicated to education. The long way of the cross lasted eleven years. Pope Leo XIII proposed an "agreement." I consented to it and begged for "forgiveness from the Monsignor" in a letter dated July 2, 1882.

Our Church is not a Church of saints, but a holy Church, at the same time poor because of its sinners and magnificent because of its ceremonies. Beneath its wrinkles, I always found the dignified and radiant face of my holy mother, the Church of Jesus Christ, who sanctifies, at all times, its children.

I BELIEVE IN THE APOSTOLIC CHURCH

The Church is apostolic. The pope, the Holy Father, is the direct successor of Peter, the head of the apostles. The pope, according to Saint Ignatius of Loyola, is the "master of all of Christ's harvests," the key to the vault of unity. Whoever is united to the pope is united to Jesus Christ, whoever breaks with this connection is shipwrecked.

United closely to the pope, I am actively committed, as a priest in the diocese of Turin, in this harvest of the Church, our mother. To a new bishop, I recommended: "take special care of the sick, the old people, and the poor children; tread carefully when making changes in the personnel of your predecessor; do your best to win the esteem and affection of ecclesiastical authorities of the diocese who believe they had been forgotten when you were chosen over them."

"Souls, and neither money nor accolades"—that is what I told my first missionaries when they left for far-off Argentina. "Take special care of the sick, children, old people, and the poor; and you will receive blessings from God and benevolence from man. Be respectful towards all of the civil and religious authorities. Take care of your health. Work, but only according to your strength. Love each other, counsel each other, and correct each other mutually, but never have envy or spite for each other. Furthermore, may the good of one be the good of all. May the worries and sufferings of one become the worries and sufferings of all; and may each of you be strong enough to keep these far from you, or at least, keep them at bay."

A short time before leaving this earth, I wrote to a missionary in Patagonia: "These are perhaps the last words from the friend of your soul. Remember that you must always respond to the increasing calls of your mother: 'Your mother who is the Church of God' (Saint Jerome)."

And here, my friends, is my prayer to this mother most holy:

Praise be the Church,
this great mother at the knees of whom
I learned God's alphabet,
by first spelling each letter, then forming
the words of life that inspired all of my works:
happiness, tenderness, trust, joy, gentleness,
boldness, and holiness.
Praise be this fruitful mother
who gives us life through the sacraments
of Christ the Savior.
Praise it for the living bread,

and for forgiveness which makes a new sap
rise in us for a springtime of the heart.
Praise it for the saints of heaven and earth,
for Mary, the mother of the Church,
queen of the apostles, help of Christians,
attentive shepherdess who watches over
my work and makes saints arise amongst the youth.
The Church, universal mother,
opens a great mantle to all,
to the small as well as the adults,
to the ignorant as well as to the wise,
to those excluded as well as people
of all races and all colors.
It is a patient mother who is always
beginning its work of slow education,
going over, one by one, the threads of unity
which its children have always broken.
It is an ardent mother who sends witnesses
across the earth and who supports the faith
of our first missionaries of Patagonia.
It is a strong mother who exhorts us to fight
for justice and truth and supports our courage
against the enemy who prowls
with the intent of losing us.
It is the praying mother of the fire of Pentecost.
Praised be you who is loved
by the master of the universe,
acquainted with his secrets.
You, who, thanks to our night is bathed in light.
You who gives us, each day,
the One who rejoices in our youth.
Holy mother! Mother of the family of God,
be praised forever!

REFLECTION QUESTIONS

What is my perception of the Church? What shapes this perception? If my experience of the Church is less than the ideal I read about, what steps can I take to rejuvenate the Church (at the parish level, at the local level) into the reality Don Bosco knew it as? Do I participate in the sacraments of the church on a regular basis? Am I active in the Church and its organizations? Do I seek to bring others into the Church? Or, if they already members, do I seek to inspire them to be more active members of the Body of Christ?

Mary Is Your Gentle Mother

FOCUS POINT

Mary teaches us so much. She teaches us how to be a perfect servant of God, how to say "yes" completely to the will of God. She also teaches us—as she taught Don Bosco—how to be gentle and caring in our dealings with others. As she humbly accepted the will of God at the Annunciation, as she lovingly visited her cousin Elizabeth, as she compassionately intervened at the wedding at Cana, we look to Mary as a model of responding with love to the call of God and the call of those in need. May we all seek the counsel and intervention of the Blessed Virgin Mary in our lives.

In this sanctuary of Oropa, I thought about my dear sons in Turin and said to myself: "Oh, if I could have them all here next to me, to lead them to the feet of Mary, to offer them and place them under her powerful protection, make them all like Dominic Savio and Saint Aloysius Gonzaga...." Then, I made this prayer before the miraculous altar of Mary: "Mary, bless all of our houses, keep the shadow of sin far from the hearts of our young people; be their guide, for them be the Seat of Wisdom. May they all be yours, always yours; always look upon them as your dear sons and always keep them amongst those who are devoted to you" (Don Bosco's letter to his children, Shrine of Oropa, August 6, 1863).

MARY, THE MOST GENTLE SHEPHERDESS

On the evening of my first Mass in Castelnuovo, June 10, 1841, my mother and I were traveling to the village of my birth called Becchi. At a detour in the road, we came to our family home, nestled in the greenery. At the place where I had my first prophetic dream when I was nine years old, I could no longer contain my tears and said: "How marvelous are the designs of Providence! God had truly lifted, from the sod, a poor child to place him amongst the greatest of his people!"

You may have noticed that these words have the mark of the *Magnificat*. I would have liked to prolong them today and celebrate the One who had been, as in the upper chamber, the living memorial of my work, and who has remained the vigilant shepherdess for me, the most pure and immaculate, lady of the great mantle, the helper.

Blessed are you, Lord, for Mary, our most gentle and very good mother, faithful shepherdess who consoles and counsels. When I was interviewed during my visit to Paris about the training that we were giving to the young people, I responded: "Our training can be summed up in two points: gentleness in all things, and the chapel is always open, offering all of our facilities for confession and Communion."

Gentleness, not weakness or fragility; gentleness, the virtue of the strong, "for they will inherit the earth" (Mt 5:5); the gentleness that comes from goodness and peace. I did not discover my method in scholarly books, but gathered it from the very lips of the mysterious person and from the woman in the dream I had when I was nine years old. One day, I told Pius IX about it and, at his request, I then wrote it down for my children:

I found myself in a very vast yard where many children were playing. Some of them were swearing. Upon hearing that I soon threw myself into their midst, screaming and hitting them to get them to be quiet. At that very moment, a majestic person who was richly dressed, appeared to me. He called me by name and said: "It isn't by hitting, but by gentleness and charity that you must conquer these children and make them your friends." I asked him who he was. "Ask your mother for my name." At that very moment, next to him, I saw a majestic woman clothed in a mantle, resplendent like the sun. She took me by the hand and said: "Look!" And I perceived that the children had fled. In their place there was a great number of young goats, cats, bears, and other similar beasts. "Here is your field, she told me, be humble, courageous, and strong. And what you see passing for animals, you will turn into your children." I then turned my head. And this is what I saw: where there had been these ferocious animals, there appeared as many lambs who were running and bleating around the man and this woman, as if they were celebrating. Then, she placed her hand on my head and said: "You will understand later!" This dream left a strong impression on me for my entire life.

The two people had given me some advice: "Not violence but gentleness, humility, and courage." The lady had taken me by the hand "with kindness"; she had shown me her area of interest "with her children" and she had told me: "you will understand later." The dream renewed itself after I became a priest. The lady had become the shepherdess and the sheep her mindful flock. As I wrote in my book, *Memories*: "I understood the events as they happened. This dream, which I considered to be a follow-up of the one I had when I was nine, had an effect on all my decisions."

The lady with the mantle of sunshine entered into the history of my work and gently led me.

MARY THE IMMACULATE

Blessed are you, Lord, for Mary who is all purity, all holiness, the humble servant who said "yes" without fail, transformed by the Savior she gave us!

On December 8, 1854, in Rome, Pope Pius IX proclaimed "Mary is immaculate in her conception." To my wounded boys, for the most part, in their hearts and in their bodies, I presented Mary as a witness of true love. She is all pure, my friends, all beautiful. She is like the sun, the moon, the most brilliant stars, she is the sealed fountain. The angel greeted her as being "full of grace" to show that, right from the beginning of her existence, she was without original sin and lived without sin until her death.

Today I make this prayer: "Mary, marvelous young woman, you never refused God the smallest proof of love. Your 'yes' had been without fail. You remained faithful to your word.

You dedicated yourself to your mission. That is why God chose your virginal heart to dwell among us and transformed you by his presence. Oh Mary, recipient of pure love, take us with you!"

A thirteen-year-old boy who had just arrived at my school seized this call. He was named Dominic Savio. He participated with an extreme fervor in the novena in preparation for December 8. On the evening of the feast day, he went to Mary's altar. He renewed the promises of his first Communion; then he repeated several times, word for word, the following: "Mary, I give you my heart. Make it so that it's always yours. Jesus and Mary, always be my friends. But, with your grace, make it so that I die rather than have the hardship of committing one sole mortal sin." And from that moment on, his life changed. He blossomed and reached out to others.

Three months later, I called for holiness in a Lenten sermon. Dominic replied: "Present!" He wanted to become a saint, a saint who was happy and contagious. The Immaculate Virgin had seized him. She came to lead him to the summits.

THE LADY WITH THE GREAT MANTLE

Blessed are you, Lord, for the lady with the great mantle welcomes, consoles, and protects. May she be our help and our guide to paradise!

In the book, *The Month of Mary,* I wrote: "We are the adoptive sons of Mary, that is why she loves and protects us. Let us contemplate the cross where Jesus would die. Looking at John, he said to Mary: 'Mother, here is your son.' Looking at Mary, he said to John: 'Here is your mother.' Yes, before leaving us, he wanted Mary to be our mother and for us to be her children."

Thus, I tell you, my friends, receive this most holy mother into your heart!

I built an important basilica that I dedicated to Mary, Help of Christians. Each stone—I tell you this in truth—was a favor granted by Mary. In the choir of this church there is a painting that shows her carrying Jesus, radiant, above the apostles, she is our queen. Her actions manifested themselves in the foundation of the female branch of our congregation. The beginnings of the institute, the Daughters of Our Lady, Help of Christians (1872), were very humble: a small work room in the country headed by a young peasant woman with a heart of fire, Maria Mazzarello. But the tree grew and produced fruit right away.

Allow me to praise her, this all-powerful mother, for her perpetual help. I thank her for her counsels at the crucial time when I chose my vocation. I was going to enter the Franciscan order and already registered on their list of postulants in Chieri when a fervent novena in her honor with my friend Comollo brought me peace. With confidence, I entered the seminary. I thank her for her comfort when my mother, Margaret, died. On the morning of that day, I arrived accompanied by a young mason at the shrine close to "La Consolation." I celebrated Mass and made this prayer: "Now my good mother, we are here. Your children and I are without a mother. You must take her place. A family like mine can't go on without a mother. All of my children, I entrust to you. Watch over them. Watch over their souls. Watch over them forever." And that morning, another mother took over. Her great mantle opened itself like two immense wings to tenderly protect all the poor children of Valdocco.

Finally, I give thanks for the presence of Mary, at the hours of death of numerous young people in our house. I saw Michel Magon die, this bubbly gang leader with a heart of gold, charmed from the moment of his arrival by Mary, the Seat of Wisdom. I had been witness to his joyous sleep, as he liked to call it. In the infirmary, I asked him what consoled him the most at this supreme moment. He replied: "What consoled me the most was the little that I did to honor Mary."

Magnificat! Such is the poem that I sang with you, my friends! "The servant of Mary will never perish," said Saint Alphonsus Liguori, my master. Let us be these faithful servants! Every day put one hand in that of Jesus and the other in that of Mary. And go joyously to paradise!

REFLECTION QUESTIONS

How do I seek to foster a relationship with Mary in my own life? If I am not already doing so, might I consider praying the rosary (alone or in a group) on a regular basis? Might I consider incorporating prayer sessions into my spiritual life that involve reflections focused on those areas of Scripture concerning the Blessed Virgin? Might I consult a priest, religious, or spiritual director as to what might be a suitable resource or method of prayer for increasing and deepening my devotion to Mary?

DAY SIX
Holiness Is for You

FOCUS POINT

The word *holiness* can seem quite overwhelming to some of us. When we think of holy people, we often think of saints of the Church, those men and women who lived great lives of devotion to our Lord and to whom we pray for intercession. But aren't we all called to holiness? Yes. We are all called to be holy people, called to be saints. And what does it mean to be holy? To be holy means that we choose love as our response to all that we encounter, day to day, moment to moment. It is that simple, yet very challenging. But when we keep God at the center of our thoughts and actions, holiness results.

Become a saint, you say? But we have to have the time to pray and go to Church. We have to be rich to make large donations. We must be wise to study, reflect, and contemplate.

No, that's wrong! We don't have to have a great deal of

time, nor be rich or wise. On the other hand, a lack of things to do makes one lazy, wealth leads to greed, and knowledge could favor pride. In order to become a saint we must, first and above everything else, want to.

Jesus told us: "You who are burdened by worries, if you want an inexhaustible source of satisfaction, be saints!" (John Bosco, The Lives of Saint Isidore and Saint Zita, *Turin, 1853, Preface).*

HOLINESS IS A LOVING RESPONSE

For Saint Isidore, who was a peasant, and for Saint Zita, who was a servant, holiness was a path of happiness. They replied "yes" to Jesus who called them.

My friends, are you ready to imitate them? The apostle Paul exhorts us to deliver ourselves to holiness (see Rom 6). During my life, I have met people who have given themselves in this way to God through a complete "yes." My own mother who, at the age of fifty-six, left her village to join me in Turin to serve the poor, belongs in this category. In her own home she was the queen, yet she became a servant to the most under-privileged. Father Joseph Cafasso, my friend and compatriot was the same. He impressed me through his examples and his advice. If I have done something good in my life, I owe it to him. Frequently, I've said to myself: "Are there saints among these young people, amongst these children aged twelve to twenty that we welcome to our oratories? They are generous and spontaneous. Some are wounded in their bodies, some in their hearts, but all are fervent and of good will. So, saints among us, why not?" I dared to believe it.

It was a Sunday in Lent, 1855. The children were hurrying in our church, some were going to class and others were apprentices, for the most part, in the building trades. During the homily, I prayed very hard to the Holy Spirit. I cited Saint Paul: "For this is the will of God, your sanctification..." (1 Thess 4:3), and I added to it: "God's great plan for you is holiness! I proclaim this good news today. Holiness is not a personal exploit, it's an adventure for two, a cooperative adventure. It does not mean to sculpt a statue to place it in the front of the building, but to reply to a friend who extends his hand. Everything began on the day of our baptism when our Father in heaven said: 'you are my beloved child. I have loved you forever. Be holy just as I am holy.' Are you ready to reply now? The adventure is worth it! Put yourself on the road. Holiness is heaven, today, among us."

The message was given. One boy received it. His life would be changed. Dominic Savio was thirteen years old. A spark inflamed his heart that day. I met with him a little while later. He told me: "Within me, I feel the need to make myself holy. I understand that we can get there by remaining happy. I want to give myself to the Lord forever. God wants me to be a saint, I must be a saint!" A dialogue began and I invited this boy to dwell in peace and scrupulously fulfill all of his duties at school.

I called other boys after that. Michel Magon was a small gang leader that I met by accident at a rest stop in the station close to Turin. His parish priest had pointed him out to me as "a universal disrupter, without a conscience and irresponsible." He spent sixteen months with us. The Lord had changed his life and called him home at the age of fourteen. I also admired François Besucco, a small shepherd from the Alps, who had a soul as clear as a pool of water, a heart burning with fervor. His death in the infirmary was, to the assistants, a veritable transformation. His face radiated with light. He had also said "yes."

HOLINESS BEGINS EVERY DAY

Saint Francis de Sales, wisely, wrote to Madam de Chantal: "Let us not forget the maxim of the saints who warned us that, every day, we must judge that we are beginning our advancement. We must always begin again and begin again with a good heart" (Letter dated May 1, 1615). I also explained to Dominic that his path with the Lord began again every day. Very soon, he put himself on the path. He had made a radical choice. I had, in my hands, his first Communion promises: (1) I will confess very often and take Communion as many times as my confessor will allow; (2) I want to sanctify the feast days; (3) my friends will be Jesus and Mary; (4) death, but not sin. These resolutions, which he often repeated, would, in so many words, become the rules for his actions until the end of his life.

At the age of thirteen, on December 8, 1854, the day when Pope Pius IX proclaimed Mary to have been immaculate from her conception, Dominic renewed his decision: "Mary, I give my heart to you. Make it so that it will always be yours. Jesus, Mary, always be my friends." This dedication prepared the ground that, three months later, would receive the call to holiness. The seeds had fallen on fertile ground. Quickly, they would bring fruit.

I said to Dominic: "In order to be a saint, be joyful every day." When he arrived at the Oratory, he was worried. But a contagious smile quickly lit up his face. To a new arrival named Gavio, he confided: "Here, holiness consists of us being joyous always." I said to Dominic: "In order to be a saint, be faithful to your duties. Respect your agenda, apply yourself, give yourself completely to the games in the yard, give time to others, be fervent in prayer." I told him: "In order to be a saint, accept all of the disagreements of daily life." He wanted to put woodchips in his bed and use only one blanket. I observed: "Cover yourself well. Put on gloves to care for your chilblains (a painful itching and swelling of the skin on the hands and feet caused by exposure to the cold and poor circulation). With patience, withstand the heat, cold, snow, fatigue, and sickness. Do you know what penance Jesus preferred? Obedience in all things. That is the secret to peace."

Thus Dominic progressed from day to day, faithful to his work, offered to God as a loving response.

HOLINESS IS CONTAGIOUS

"Our God is a consuming fire" (Heb 12:29). God wants us to be contagious apostles. This is the path that I proposed to Dominic:

BE AN APOSTLE

The first thing I counseled him to do to become a saint was to work, with all of his strength, to win souls for God, for there is nothing holier in this world than to cooperate for the good of the souls that Jesus redeemed by shedding his blood to the very last drop.

BE OF SERVICE

Give your time to others, be attentive to their needs and to their worries, bring them the flower of your smile. Dominic went to offer his services at the infirmary. He was a tutor for those who lagged behind. Spontaneously, he helped his friends in the little daily tasks: waxing the shoes, brushing the clothes.... "Each one does what he can," he repeated. "I can't do big things, but what I can do I will do for the Lord; I hope that, in his infinite goodness, God will accept the poor actions I offer him."

BE AN ARTISAN OF PEACE

One day, two boys decided to fight each other by throwing stones after a violent dispute. They went towards an empty lot. Dominic followed them. "Throw the first stone at me!" he cried to the more angry of the two and he showed them the small crucifix he wore around his neck. The two fighters dropped their arms. Another time, he called to order a rowdy person who was throwing snowballs at the young people who were warming themselves around a stove. Vexed, the boy rushed at Dominic and violently slapped him. Dominic didn't say a word. He turned red and remained calm.

HAVE CONFIDENCE IN JESUS AND MARY

In order to be strong, we must maintain our strength. From the time of his arrival at the Oratory, I said to Dominic: "Take Communion and visit Jesus in the Eucharist; receive forgiveness and have confidence in Mary." The Eucharist was his strength. He said, his eyes filled with light, "I am only missing one thing here on earth: contemplating, face to face, the One whom I see in faith and adore today on the altar."

BE A GATHERER

Finally, I showed him the path of the apostolate. Gather your friends. Be apostles together. Unite yourselves, become a team. "Unity creates strength." "A triple thread is stronger than a single one." On December 8, 1855, in the year when I made the call to holiness, he gathered his best friends, around fifteen, and together they founded the Company of the Immaculate, a dynamic team of generous and ardent boys. These first companions would become the Salesians. Dominic had been their inspiration. He wanted to be a missionary, but his fragile health cut his dream short. He died at the age of fifteen. With all of his strength, he threw himself into following in the footsteps of Christ, trying to grasp him, for Christ was his life, and to die for him was "gain" (Phil 1:21). Thus, holiness is possible at all ages. Saints, yesterday as well as today, exist and are very alive. All we have to do is love!

REFLECTION QUESTIONS

What is my understanding of holiness? Do I think only of great acts of devotion or perfect people as I consider what it means to be holy? What little things do I do in my daily life that keep my mind and heart centered on God? What other practices might I incorporate into my spiritual life to aid me in maintaining a "loving response" to every situation and every person I encounter each day and from moment to moment? What points of holiness from the list Don Bosco gave to Dominic Savio might I seek to work on in the coming days?

DAY SEVEN
Live in Happiness

FOCUS POINT

God wants us to be happy, to live joyously. We are made to be happy, to serve God in joy, to serve each other in happiness. God gives us everything we need. We are saved by Jesus Christ. There is no reason to be sad or to approach our work or duty with anything less than joy. If we are not happy in our lives, we must refocus ourselves on the Lord; if we are unhappy at the present time, we are focusing on those things that are less than God, that cannot fulfill us, that leave us without peace, wanting for more, full of anxiety and worry.

As a young priest, I wrote the following words on one of the bookmarks in my breviary: "I know that there is nothing better...than to be happy and to...take pleasure in all (our) toil" (Eccl 3:12–13). That is the golden rule of which I never lost sight. When Dominic came to see me to receive some ad-

vice after my sermon about holiness, I answered the following on the spot: "Be happy and be an apostle." Today, my friends, I invite you to discover this "complete joy" (see Jn 15:11) that Jesus gives us.

"O COME...LET US MAKE A JOYFUL NOISE" (PS 95:1)

The Psalms let the joy of life burst forth. "Young men and women alike, old and young together!" (Ps 148:12), "clap your hands, dance, sing, shout, take up your instruments...and praise the name of the Lord!" All of creation unites for this concert. This simple joy sings in me with a happy disposition which I think I received from my mother. One evening, a little after we moved to Turin, always in a good mood, she laughingly sang this to me:

To those who make fun of us, shame.
Strangers who haven't a cent to their name!

I had a quick wit and the gift to sow joy. I was passionate about games, especially those that offered pleasure. During my childhood, I had seen the playfulness of little kittens and puppies, and heard the songs of the black-headed larks. To play is to rejoice.

I often accompanied my mother to the markets and studied even the smallest gestures made by the jugglers and tumblers. Would you believe it? At the age of twelve, I did magic tricks and various acrobatic moves, just like a professional.

Games are a means of relaxation for the body, joy for the spirit, and a source of equilibrium and good health. At an early age, I quoted and adopted the words of Saint Philip Neri, the apostle of young people: "Run, jump, relax; but, above all, no sinning!" And I repeated: run, jump, and go out and breathe in the pure air! Walks and trips, music and theater enchanted my fledglings! Each one assumed his place in the family of Valdocco. Joy created bonds and opened hearts like flower buds in the April sunshine.

"REJOICE ALWAYS" (SEE PHIL 4:4)

"Rejoice in the Lord always; again I will say, Rejoice" (Phil 4:4). Saint Paul showed us the meaning of perfect joy. Joy that has its source in the heart of God cannot be ephemeral. It is God who gives it to us so that our lives will blossom. His joy took the first steps.

JOY IS BORN FROM GOD

See, my friends, how God's joy has come to the world. At Christmas, it sings of the birth of the Savior; the joy of the angels and shepherds, the joy of Mary in her *Magnificat*, the joy of Simon who welcomes the Infant. The joy of believing and celebrating Emmanuel (God made man). Before leaving those close to him, Jesus said: "I have said these things to you so that my joy may be in you, and that your joy may be complete" (Jn 15:11). Welcome this complete joy that comes to us from God. I wrote, in *The Educated Young Man*: "Our God is the God of joy!" Joy is the offspring of love.

JOY IS FULL OF WONDER

During my childhood, in the clear mornings of springtime, I looked in awe at the chain of glaciers in the Alps that sparkled in the rising sun.

JOY IS PEACEFUL

Don Cafasso said: "May nothing bother you!" His face was radiant and peaceful. He breathed in God's joy. One day, Dominic Savio said to me: "True joy is born from peace in the heart and tranquillity of the soul." Are joy and peace not the "fruit" of the Holy Spirit (see Gal 5:22)? I wrote to a boy on vacation: "be joyful, but may your joy be authentic, like that of a conscience that is pure of all sin." Joy and peace are siblings, they are earned together. Joy in the heart is a joyful heart, and peace in the heart is a peaceful heart.

JOY IS WARM

It seals friendships and makes them shine. Two friendships had illuminated my life. Comollo, a college friend, had a temperament that was different from mine. He was gentle, but I could say that I learned to live as a Christian from him. I admired his fervor, his deprivations, and his goodness. He died at the age of twenty-three. Jonas, a young Jew, came to find me after classes at the coffee shop where I was a waiter. He was a musician. God fascinated him, he received Christian baptism and this was a great celebration. He remained my friend, a ray of sunshine in my life.

JOY IS A CELEBRATION

The history of our work is written, as one could say, from one celebration to the next. Celebrations gather people together and recreate. Secular celebrations with theater, dance, and music: a house of education without music is like a body without a soul! Liturgical celebrations in honor of the Lord, Mary and the saints, prepared for by novenas, celebrated in the ostentation of ceremonies—nothing is too beautiful for God!

"WORSHIP THE LORD WITH GLADNESS" (PS 100:2)

In the book, *The Educated Young Man*, I associated joy to the service of the Lord, charity-love. The hymn to charity of Saint Paul is, for the Christian, a hymn to joy in our daily life.

JOY IS ATTENTIVE

My mother excelled in the art of pleasing our orphans. I still hear their demands: "Mama, an apple! Mama, I don't have any more tissue! I ripped my pants!" With a smile, discreetly, she was always attentive. I remember the afternoon snacks on the feast of Saint Anne, the patroness of the masons of the first Oratory. With my superior from Convitto, we received them. They were served coffee, chocolate, croissants, brioches, and all types of cookies. They were elated. In my pockets, I always had a "stash" of candies, medals, and holy images. Little gifts spread joy: a few bottles of vermouth for my benefactors in Toulon, or a bunch of grapes picked from my balcony for my visitors. The words of the Lord are true: "It is more blessed to give than to receive" (Acts 20:35).

JOY IS PATIENT

At the age of fifty-eight, when I was seriously ill, I wrote to a collaborator: "The eye doctors that were consulted brought down the following verdict: right eye—very little hope; left eye— can maintain the status quo, on the condition that I refrain from reading and writing. Therefore, I must eat, drink, sleep, and exercise well, and if I do that, I will get better." We must patiently "get better" all the way to the end. During my very last illness, half paralyzed, I again wrote a bad poem, in Piedmontese (my native dialect), to encourage my poor legs which no longer wanted to carry me!

JOY IS TRUSTING

My infirmities worsened as I aged. I confided to a Salesian missionary in Argentina: "Don't worry if I don't write. I am nearly blind and barely able to walk, write, and speak. What do you expect? I am old and it's the will of God! But every day, I pray for you, for all of my sons, and I want all of you to willingly serve the Lord with holy gladness!" The cross gives birth to pure joy, it announces the dawn of Easter!

JOY GOES BEYOND DEATH

Listen to the last words of Dominic Savio, as his father reported them to me: "Now, father, I am happy. Tell everyone!" Then: "My dear father, I want to eternally sing praises to the Lord!" And also, with a smiling face: "Oh, how beautiful is what I am seeing!" That was on March 9, 1857—he was fifteen years old.

Friends, let us serve the Lord in gladness. One day, we will see him in the eternal jubilation of the saints in heaven! Jesus promised us that: "I will see you again, and your hearts will rejoice, and no one will take your joy from you" (Jn 16:22). This joy is within us. May we know how to make it blossom. It is joy that remains!

REFLECTION QUESTIONS

At what times in my life am I most filled with joy and at peace? At what times am I anxious or sad? What is it about certain situations or specific people that seem to turn me from joy to sadness? How can I find joy during these times that normally cause me to be anxious or sad? Might I make it a point to take a step back during these times and focus my attention on the Lord and the love and joy he fosters within me? Might my response to situations that usually make me sad be one of love and joy if my focus is God and not something less than God?

DAY EIGHT

Work in Your Own Field

FOCUS POINT

Wherever we are, right now, we are called to do God's work. We don't have to join a church group to do our part, or even be part of an organized charity (although those are both good things to do)—we can do God's work right here, right now. God's work need not be separated from the ordinary. In fact, that's exactly where it is needed the most. Jesus came to the poorest and neediest, the most ordinary people in creation. He came to them because they were crying out for his love. It is the same with those people and places today where the light of God does not shine. If we are there with these people in need, we can work to let the love of God shine through us.

Dear young people, laziness is the main trap used to tempt you by the devil. It is the mother of all vices. Be convinced that man was born to work; if he doesn't work, he will be out of the

*game. You don't have to be busy from morning to night with-
out taking a breath.... Don't waste your time, for time is a
treasure. You don't know if you will live a long life or have the
time to gain merits for heaven. Scripture says: "Train children
in the right way, and when old, they will not stray" (Prov 22:6),
which means: if we seek true happiness during our childhood,
we will be virtuous until a ripe old age (John Bosco,* The Educated Young Man, *Turin, 1847, Introduction).*

SOW YOUR FIELD

At our house, we had to work to live. My mother provided the
example. I still hear her native words in Piedmontese: "A bad
washerwoman will never find a good stone"; and "Whoever
doesn't work, won't eat." She was as busy as a bee, and we
imitated her. My first field was our field in Becchi. I seeded and
harvested; I trimmed the vines, harvested the bunches of grapes,
picked the grapes, and pressed them. I also hired myself out as
a farm hand for two years.

For ten years, I was a serious student. At the same time, I
had to earn my living to pay my way. I was a waiter in a coffee
shop, I tailored suits, and repaired shoes. During my vacations
from the seminary, I sewed footwear and worked iron and
wood. This adeptness with my hands served me well at the
beginning of my work, when I had to do everything myself.
When I had become a priest, losing no time, I visited the prisons with my friend and master. I was chaplain of a girl's school.
At the same time, I was meeting with the young people on their
work sites, I made contact with their employers and defended
their rights through apprenticeship contracts. Then came the
oratories, the young people's home in Valdocco.

Work became "the weapon and the pride" of my children,

and a path to holiness. To the Salesians, I said: "Work and temperance will make our congregation flourish. Seeking the easy way will signify death.... I heard that the Salesians work for the Church right up until their last breath.... Whenever a Salesian dies for the salvation of souls, our congregation will have won a great victory."

I vigorously urged the young people to be courageous sowers.

To you, Maria, who organized a working room with your friends in your village, and who welcomed adolescent girls in difficulty, I said: "Work with ardor, God will bless you. The little seed of your work will become a great tree!"

To you, Dominic Savio, I said: "Be attentive to your schoolwork. You want to become a saint right now; use your time well. Work under God's gaze. You will find peace of heart and the joy of service."

To Ottavio, the tailor, I said: "Pay attention to your duties; have confidence in your employers. Let us work together for the happiness of all. Let us work for paradise."

To Emmanuel, who was preparing for his first Communion, I said: "I recommend: (1) obedience to your parents and your other superiors; (2) accuracy in your schoolwork—don't groan about it."

To Joseph, the young teacher, discouraged with his students, I said: "Remain faithful to your responsibilities, (...) always try to encourage them. Never humiliate them. Congratulate them when it is appropriate, but never scorn them. At the very most, express your displeasure as a means of punishment."

To all of you, I say, be good sowers. "Whatever your task, put yourselves into it, as if it is done for the Lord" (Col 3:23).

TAKE YOUR TIME

It is written in the Bible: "For everything there is a season, and a time for every matter under heaven…a time to plant, and a time to pluck up what is planted; a time to weep, and a time to laugh…" (Eccl 3:1–4). Don Cafasso repeated, with his lovely smile, "Each minute is a treasure." There is a time for each thing. Let us use our time well. It is golden in the currency of eternity. Listen, my friends.

A TIME TO GROW AND A TIME TO MAKE SOMETHING GROW

During my childhood, in the spring, I liked to watch the green sprouts that came from the seeds I planted that would later produce the harvest in the summer. This is my parable of the Grain of Wheat: the seed, thrown onto the ground, in the autumn, is but only one minute seed lost in the soil. Small and frail, it already carries the heavy, golden grain of the harvest to come inside of it. In order to ripen, it needs the long sleep of winter, to die in the soil in order to free the fine stem of green. The seed is not yet the golden grain, yet the grain of wheat is already there. The rain, sun, light, and heat bring it to maturity. It takes time to grow, it must have time to ripen into a grain. The same analogy holds for the kingdom of God; a seed ripens, and a child matures. The adult is already there, inside of him. By dying to his egoism and his fears, he will come to be an adult, able to, himself, give a hundredfold. Doesn't this parable make you think of education? A time to plant seeds, a time to grow in tenderness and confidence, and, finally, a time to harvest.

A TIME TO LIVE AND A TIME TO DIE

Upon arriving at the seminary, my curiosity was aroused by the solar clock that dominated the yard. On it, I read: "The hours pass slowly for gloomy spirits, they pass quickly for those with joyous hearts." I immediately said to my friend, "This is my plan: let us be happy and the time will pass quickly!" I put joy at the heart of education: joy through games, joy for celebrations, the joy of existence and of living together!

But like the shadow that slowly draws its curve on the solar clock, our lives run out every day until their twilight. The hour of our death approaches, little by little. Let us hold our beacon, watching for the dawn, for the Master is coming to meet us!

BE A WORKER FOR THE HARVEST

If, at times, "one sows and another reaps" (Jn 4:37), we are all involved in the harvest. We all receive the reward of "eternal life" (Jn 4:36).

THE WORKER DESERVES HIS WAGES

Jesus underlined it in the parable of the Laborers of the Vineyard (see Mt 20): all of the laborers received the same wage, those who started work later in the day as well as those who worked all day. The salary assured them of their daily bread, but "anyone unwilling to work should not eat" (2 Thess 3:10).

WORK IS PRAYER

Maria Mazzarello repeated to her companions: "Friends, have confidence, each stitch is an act of love"—a love that is an offering. To a young Salesian missionary in Buenos Aires, I wrote: "Work! But work for the love of Jesus. Suffer rather than break with charity." To Don Rua, I made this recommendation: "Remind the members of our Society that for the love of our Master, each person must work, obey, and abandon all that he possessed in the world."

WORK IS THE ROAD TO HOLINESS

Holiness is expressed through apostolic zeal. It is also seen in the exercise of our responsibilities in the Church. If we are happy harvesters, we will draw other workers into God's field. Holiness is contagious.

My friends, let us work in our own field, the one where God planted us so we would flourish and bring fruit. When I founded our third order, I cited Saint Paul: "For we are God's servants, working together; you are God's field, God's building" (1 Cor 3:9). Let us remain these servants of God, inventive and bold.

REFLECTION QUESTIONS

Do I seek to do God's work wherever I happen to find myself? Or do I separate certain parts of my life, keeping my love for God in one area and living my life apart from God (or not bringing him up) in another area? How do I spend my leisure time? Do I spend too much time watching television or gossiping? Do I find my leisure time leads me to give in to temptation? Might I consider filling my "down time" with service to God? Might I seek out those activities that suit my interests, hobbies, and talents, and also serve to do God's work in the process?

DAY NINE

One Heart, One Family

FOCUS POINT

As members of the Body of Christ, we are the people of God. We are one family, baptized in the name of our Lord. Even beyond the Church, we are united with all of creation; all men and women are part of the family of God's creation. Keeping this in mind, we must not be afraid to reach out to others— family, friends, or strangers. We must imitate Jesus in this way. He loved everyone he encountered, regardless of their social standing, their beliefs, or their attitudes towards him. We are called to love everyone, because everyone is a part of our family.

To Don Rua and all the other sons who loved Saint Francis de Sales and lived in Turin:

Our Society will probably, in a short time, be definitively approved; I will also have to speak to my beloved sons fre-

*quently. Not always being able to do this in person, I will strive
to do it in the form of letters.*

*Oh, if our brothers enter the Society out of love and to
serve Jesus Christ all the way to the end, our houses will certainly become a true earthly paradise. Peace and harmony will
reign amongst members of each family; charity will be the daily
attitude for those who command it, obedience and respect will
precede all interventions, actions, and even the thoughts of the
superiors. In all, we will have a family of brothers, assembled
around their father to promote the glory of God and to then
go, one day, to love and bless him in the immense glory of the
blessed ones in heaven.*

*May God fulfill you, may God bless you, and may the
grace of the Lord sanctify your actions and help you to perse-
vere in goodness (John Bosco, priest, Turin, June 9, 1867, Pentecost).*

YOU ARE THE APPLE OF MY EYE

I didn't know the loving glance of a father, perhaps that is why
I sought other glances to recognize and love me.

When I was an adolescent, I sought some attention from
my parish priest and his vicar. I met them often on the road. I
waved at them from afar, but as dignified as they were, they
were satisfied just to return my wave and go on their way. I
cried over it and said to myself: "Later, if I become a priest, I
will go up to the children to say something nice to them." I
was seeking just a little attention....

I found some brothers. In the heart of the only son of a
widow, who had been one of our collaborators, I saw trust:
"You wrote me that the news about Mama was very serious.
No matter what happens in the future, you know that Don

Bosco promises you, and your mother, that he will act as your father, particularly for your soul." To my dear sons in Mirabello College in Piedmont, for Christmas, 1864, I addressed these lines: "I thank you for your tokens of friendship. You are the apples of my eye. I would like you to give me your hearts so that, each day, I can offer them at Mass." I replied the following to the new year's wishes from the students of Lanzo College: "When I went to see you, you enchanted me by your benevolence and graciousness, you captivated my spirit through your piety. I still have this poor heart, from which you have stolen all my affections. Yet, your letter, signed by two hundred friendly and very dear hands, took possession of all of this heart where nothing now remains, other than a vivid desire to love you in the Lord, to do good for you, and to save your souls."

YOU ARE A SINGLE BEE HIVE

Right from the origins of our family in Valdocco, a new tradition came into being: the "evening chat." It was a simple and cordial conversation where the father addresses his sons to instruct, sanctify, and also amuse them.

One of these evening chats, in February 1864, which one of my listeners transcribed, could have been entitled "the parable of the Bee Hive":

My friends, let us take ourselves into one of our villages in the springtime. We discover a field covered with flowers, shining under the rays of the sun. Here is a bee hive, brimming with life. Each bee has his own job. The queen gathers them and assures their unity and fruitfulness. The workers fly from flower to flower and gather the precious nectar; other bees keep watch, building the honeycombs, feeding the larvae. Each works for the good of the others. Each produces the honey, the daily bread of this great family. Each one obeys. Imitate the bees in their obedience to the queen; that is, obey the rules proposed by your masters. Without obedience, there is no unity possible; disorder comes to be and criticism divides. Honey nourishes. Imitate the bees who produce the honey. Honey is our treat and, at times, it heals us. Honey is the result of diligent work. That is your work in class and in the workshop. Honey is the joy you sow in your play, at the theater and in our celebrations; it is the fervor of your prayers; it is the gentleness and peace that creates, in our gathered family, a rainbow of light.

When our family swarmed to Argentina, I had to envision never seeing my beloved sons again. How could I maintain the same spirit there that I had here? To one of them, a promising priest, I addressed this message: "I would like to go, myself, to hold a conference about the Salesian spirit which must drive and guide our actions. Never speak humiliating words or severe reproaches in the presence of another person. May each class resonate with words of gentleness, charity, and patience. May each Salesian make friends with everyone, never seek vengeance; and may he be quick to forgive. Gentleness in speech, actions, and advice to others allows one and all to be winners."

"YOU ARE ROOTED IN LOVE" (EPH 3:17)

You ask me where the affection comes from that permits me to teach. The affection comes from the very heart of God who is infinite love. This love is given to us through baptism; like a kind of tree sap, it mounts and nourishes. It allows one to welcome and trust. "If the root is holy, the branches also are holy...remember that it is not you that support the root, but the root that supports you" (Rom 11:16, 18). We are grafted onto Christ, we are "rooted in love."

The secret of education rests on love-charity: "love is patient...bears all things, believes all things, hopes all things, endures all things" (1 Cor 13:4, 7). I explained this in two simple principles.

First, if there is no affection, there is no trust. I said to my boys: "You are young. It is enough that you are young for me to love you. You will not find anyone who loves you in Jesus Christ and wants your happiness more than I do." I also added: "Consider that I was all yours, day and night, morning and evening, all the time. I study for you, I work for you, I live for you and am ready to give my life for you."

The young people understood. We grow only for and through those by whom we are loved. When a youth in difficulty meets a man or woman who is ready to give their life for him, he enters that relationship in trust and grows. Love creates trust.

Finally, without trust, there is no education. My mother helped me through her trust when I was an adolescent. In order to buy the necessary material for my magic tricks, I needed money. I picked mushrooms, ferns, and herbs in order to sell them...you will ask me: did my mother approve? I answer that she sought only good things for me. In her, I had unlimited confidence and trust. She knew everything, nothing escaped her, but she let me do it. Without her permission, I wouldn't have budged. From my mother, I learned to live the principles that I would later formulate, that created the spirit of our family: affection, reason, and religion.

REFLECTION QUESTIONS

From my experience, do I see the Church as being one family, a family of love and trust? If not, what can I do to foster a healthy familial life in my own parish? Do I struggle to find the courage to break down those boundaries that keep me from reaching out to friends or strangers in need? Might I ask for the grace to move outside of my fears, and love according to the Gospel model, in imitation of Jesus Christ? Do I pray regularly for a desire rooted in God the Father to serve others, to foster trust in the Church family, and love as I have been loved?

DAY TEN

Go to All Others

We are called to proclaim the Gospel to the world, to those who need to hear it the most—the poor, those in prison, children. It is rare in this day and age to see someone publicly speaking up for what they believe in. Many say that God and "God talk" should be a private issue, but God himself calls us to proclaim his holy Word by our words and by our actions. We needn't feel any shame or embarrassment for doing the will of God in this regard, and we should let no one make us feel that way by their disapproving talk and angry glances. There are people who need to hear the Good News, and they need to hear it from us!

Don Cafasso invited me to accompany him to the prisons. Thus, I learned, very early on, to what degree man's malice and misery could reach. The sight of these young people, aged twelve to eighteen, healthy, robust, lively spirited, but reduced to idleness, eaten by vermin, for me, was horrible. What stupefied me further was that many of them, once released from prison with good intentions, returned just a few days later. Who knew, I thought, if these young people had a friend on the outside who was interested in helping and teaching them? Who knew if they wouldn't be interested in being saved? I decided to become this friend!

I made this part of my reflections to Don Cafasso. With his counsel, I looked into how to make this project a reality, by totally entrusting its success to the grace of God (John Bosco, Autobiographical Memories, 1835–1845*).*

LORD, GIVE ME THE SOULS AND KEEP THE REST

That is the motto I chose for my ordination as a priest at the age of twenty-six. According to the Bible, these were the words of the King of Sodom to Abraham at the time of the conquest of Cana: "Give me the persons but take the goods for yourself" (Gen 14:21). I often repeated them in the following prayer: "Lord, give me the souls and keep the rest"—souls, that is, living people, men and women in all conditions, at all ages, of all races; rich and poor, healthy and ill, above all, the youth, those who are successful and those who fail, those who are marginalized. Lord, these souls don't belong to me, but to you. You entrusted them to me. I protected them, I served them, I offered them for your glory. All the rest, my health, my recreation, my personal interests, count for nothing. That is only "fluff"! I seek only you.

This motto was written on my office walls. Dominic Savio noticed it when he came to the Oratory. After reflection, he said to me: "I understand; here we don't deal with money but with souls. I hope that my soul will be part of these dealings." A short while after my sermon on holiness, he asked me: "Make me a saint right now!" My answer wasn't at all complicated: "Be happy and go to others, go to all other people." And he opened himself to his friends. I heard him repeat the following many times: "Oh, if I could only win all of my companions for God!" He became interested in those who were the most isolated, the most deprived. He entertained them with anecdotes and helped them with their studies. When illness struck, they all wanted him as their nurse. Savio repeated: "I want to be a missionary." Every day, he offered a prayer for this intention, and every week, Communion. I happened to hear him shout: "How many people in England await our help! If I was healthy and virtuous, I would go there, preach, and make conversions."

Sensing his approaching demise, Dominic confided to his friends: "I must run, otherwise death will surprise me on the path." On his lips, do we not find the following words of Jesus: "Walk while you have the light, so that the darkness may not overtake you…" (Jn 12:35)? Lord, give us souls! I reminded our missionaries: "Seek souls, not money; honors, not rewards."

THE POOR ARE MY FRIENDS

It is not always easy to go with the poor. One day, Don Cafasso invited me to accompany him to an execution. During his lifetime, he had tended to the souls of sixty-seven condemned prisoners. But can you see me there? I couldn't take the shock. I fainted. The emotion was too much for me.

However, I visited these prisoners for many years in their prisons. In Paris, in the church dedicated to the Magdalene, I said to the people who were listening to me: "It was in the prisons of Turin that I understood the necessity for my work." And today, I add: the revelation of my mission.

In 1841, Turin had about 130,000 inhabitants, of which approximately half were illiterate. What distress, what hidden misery! I was seized by the cry of the poorest of them. On one of the bookmarks in my breviary I wrote: "My son, do not deprive the poor of the alms that you owe them, and do not turn your eyes away from the indigent" (see Eccl 3). I began to see them as friends and brothers. I recognized the face of the Lord along my road.

It was Jesus who was suffering in these delinquents in "La Générale," a prison for young people. It was he who I met in the sick in the Cottolingo hospital, or in the orphanage where I was the chaplain for two years. He was there on my path and he called to me. I swore I would dedicate myself to the poor! And when the Marchioness Barolo asked me to choose between "her girls" and "my vagabonds," I didn't hesitate for a moment! To a friend, I wrote: "In things that pertain to young people in danger, or which serve to win souls for God, I forge ahead, even to the point of recklessness!"

LET US COOPERATE WITH GOD

These words from Saint Augustine were familiar to me: "Of divine things, the most divine is to cooperate with God for the salvation of souls."

I had the gift of gathering people together. As a child, I was already captivating an audience of all ages with my stories that lasted up to five or six hours, in a barn in our little hamlet. Throughout my life, I united young people and people of all conditions. I taught and, by teaching, I founded. My children were born on the very soil of my mission. I involved lay religious (coadjutors)—I founded an order of cooperators with lay people and priests who lived the Gospel in the spirit of our

Salesian family (Union of Cooperator Salesians—founded in 1875).

Together, in service to the Church, we became "cooperators for God," for "we are God's field, the house he built." Thus, around me I saw the birth of educational, financial, and spiritual cooperation, grouping the sick and shut-ins in prayer and offering for their suffering. I, myself, participated in Christ's suffering, knowing that we must "suffer with him in order to rejoice with him in paradise." I experienced the political and social upheavals of 1848. One day, I found myself alone with four hundred young people. All of my collaborators had abandoned me. I had been slandered and accused of foolishness. Two canons came to get me to throw me in jail. I sent them away in the very buggy in which they came to collect me! I confronted bandits, and I foiled around fifteen attempts on my life. Without my dear Grigo, my providential dog, I would have succumbed to these attempts. I suffered harassment by the police. I knew sleepless nights, uncomfortable trips, and long waits in antechambers in order to get signatures and agreements. I endured infirmities and illnesses, and all the thorns on the road here on earth! Jesus and his holy mother helped me. I fought the good fight, and, like the apostle, "aspired to the crown" of the One who "conquered the world!" (Jn 16:33).

My friends, on my little desk in Valdocco, I again see the globe that's still there. Often, I stare at it and, moved, clutch it tightly in my hands. With my eyes turned towards the crucifix, I pray: "Ah, if we could, in the spark of our charity, hold the whole world in our hands to lead them to the Church and to God!" Love "believes all things, hopes all things…never ends" (1 Cor 13:7, 8).

REFLECTION QUESTIONS

How do I feel about proclaiming the Good News to a stranger or a group of people who need to hear it? Does this prospect make me anxious? Do I feel as if I might seem to be meddling in someone else's business when an opportunity to proclaim the Gospel arises? Might I pray for the courage to preach the Good News to those people who need to hear it when the opportunity presents itself? Might I even pray for the courage to seek out these situations where my witness to the Gospel will make a positive impact on someone's life?

DAY ELEVEN

Walk in My Presence

FOCUS POINT

God wants us with him always. He is with us at all times, but it is up to us to recognize him. We must keep God in our hearts and in our thoughts. Simple practices of devotion and regular prayer make this possible. When we keep God in our hearts and in our thoughts at all times, we begin to see him in many different places, in many different people. Then our lives are even more joyous, because we see God all around us and he fills us with his love and peace. But we must make the effort to turn our attention to him.

The Word of God is called the Light because it illuminates man and directs him to believe, to act, and to love. It is the Light because, if it is well explained and taught, it shows man the road he must follow in order to have a blessed life. It is the Light because it calms man's passions, the true shadows of the

*soul, very thick and dangerous, which can only be dissipated
by the Word of God. It is the Light because, if it is well preached,
it spreads the clarity of divine grace into the hearts of the listeners and makes them know the truths of the faith (John Bosco,*
The Catholic in This Century, *Turin, 1883).*

SPEAK LORD, YOUR SERVANT IS LISTENING

God spoke in order to question Abraham, the Father of the
Believers. He said to him: "I am God Almighty; walk before
me and be blameless" (Gen 17:1). Abraham asked for no ex-
planation. "By faith Abraham obeyed when he was called to
set out for a place...not knowing where he was going" (Heb
11:8). He believed. The Word had been the light on his road.
My friends, may this light be a meeting with God for you today.

When I had been a priest for six years, I noticed this reflection during a retreat: "Prayer to a priest is like water to a fish,
air to a bird, and a stream for a deer. The person who prays is
like someone on a journey to see the king." To pray is to go
meet the King of kings; to contemplate his face, to welcome his
counsels, to entrust him with our projects and requests, and
put ourselves at his service. Samuel met the Lord this way. Three
times the voice of God rang out in the night, three times the
child got up and replied: "Speak, Lord, for your servant is listening" (1 Sam 3:9). My friends, let us imitate this attitude of a
servant who is attentive, faithful, and humble.

A servant is attentive to the words and actions of the king.
Samuel hears the Lord's words; they wake him up and awaken
his prayer: "Speak, Lord!" On one of the bookmarks in my
breviary, I wrote down this thought which has been attributed
to Saint Bernard: "Tirelessly read the Word of God; through it,

you will know the road to follow and the dangers to avoid." The Word of God is light and nourishment. It is not limited to the holy Scriptures, it is also revealed through the catechism, sermons, teachings of the Church, the lives of the saints, and all of God's witnesses. Through it, God speaks to us and invites us to pray. "I am standing at the door, knocking" (Rev 3:20).

The servant is faithful. Like Samuel, he answers his divine King without reservation or hesitation: "Here I am!" This faithfulness to prayer left its mark at certain important stages of my life. When I was fourteen, a priest showed me the way, each day, to do a meditation or a short spiritual reading. That was a great help. At the age of twenty, when I took the habit, I promised to do a little meditation and spiritual reading every day. Then, when I was ordained a priest, I decided to dedicate some time daily to meditation, spiritual reading, and a visit to the Blessed Sacrament; I resolved to prepare myself for Mass for fifteen minutes and to follow it with fifteen minutes of thanksgiving. During my lifetime, whenever it was possible, I was faithful to these resolutions.

The servant is humble. Like Samuel, he put himself at the disposal of his king to serve him and to offer him his humble duties of the day. Do you know the Merchant's Meditation? I presented it to my sons during a retreat. Whoever can't do methodological meditation, because of a trip, a job, or business that can't be put off, will at least be able to do the meditation that I call "the merchant's." Merchants always think of their business. They think of buying and selling and making profit. They think of losses they may incur and those they have already experienced and various means to absorb them. They think of their past and future profits. Such a meditation is also an examination of conscience. In the evening, before going to bed, let us examine if we have put into practice the resolutions that we have made about a certain fault; if we are in a position of profit or loss. This is a type of spiritual accounting.

"I HAVE CALMED AND QUIETED MY SOUL, LIKE A WEANED CHILD WITH ITS MOTHER" (PS 131:2)

Jesus proclaimed: "Truly I tell you, unless you change and become like children, you will never enter the kingdom of heaven" (Mt 18:3). And I add to this: "and you will not know how to pray." Having the spirit of a child is not a question of age, but of freshness of the soul, and of conversion of the heart. Then the qualities of childhood become the qualities of prayer. This prayer is confident and generous.

THE PRAYER OF A CHILD IS CONFIDENT

There was a crucial moment at the beginning of my work on the day I gathered my children together, in a meadow, one last time, April 5, 1846—we were without a home. I made this prayer: "My God, why don't you clearly show me the place where you want me to gather my children? Oh, make me aware of it and tell me what I must do." And suddenly there arrived my savior, Pancrace Soave, who offered me a house for a shelter.

THE PRAYER OF A CHILD IS GENEROUS

On the day I took my habit in 1835, while my parish priest was dressing me with this holy habit, I made this prayer: "Oh, how many old habits must I get rid of! My God, destroy my bad habits!" And I continued, full of emotions: "Yes, my God, make it so that, from now on, I begin a new life, according to your will. May faithfulness and holiness be the constant subject of my thoughts and my actions. Amen! Mary, be the sun of my soul!"

Do we have the heart of a child to praise, give thanks, ask forgiveness, and "sing of the marvels of our God"?

"GOD, YOU ARE MY GOD, I SEEK YOU FROM DAWN" (SEE PS 63)

Jesus made his friends into watchmen. In the garden of his agony, he invited the apostles to stand watch with him. He called his friends to "keep watch and always pray." He turns each Christian into an ardent witness of prayer at all times, for all duties.

Prayers for all of the liturgical hours are offered in the book, *The Educated Young Man*. In the morning, I indicated what you would today call "a wink at the Lord": "I adore you, oh my God, and I love you with all of my heart. I thank you for having created me. I offer you all of my actions of this day." In the evening, it is a filial abandonment into the arms of God: "Forgive me, my God, for the sins I have committed and accept the little good that I may have done." To a French collaborator, Claire Louvet, I proposed this timetable for God: "Do a few things, but observe them with care. Each year: an examination of conscience regarding progress and regret for the past year. Each month: an exercise of a good death, with confession and Communion as if they had to be our last. Each week: holy confession. Pay strict attention to remembering the guidelines given by our confessor. Each day: holy Communion if possible, meditation, and examination of conscience, consideration of each day as our last."

I reminded a religious sister of a simple and practical way to remain united to God: "If you want a few matches to make the sparks of love burst forth, you will find them through spontaneous prayer in honor of the Blessed Sacrament."

Such is the road for our prayer, which is "a response of

love to the Lord who walks with us towards the homeland where true happiness awaits. My friends, have you noticed that when Moses was coming down from the mountain, he did not know that the skin of his face shone because he had been talking with God" (see Ex 34:29)? Could this happen to you? Could you return to your friends after a time of prayer with a radiant face after meeting the Lord? Could you offer them a more marvelous gift?

REFLECTION QUESTIONS

Do I turn my attention to God as often as I should? How can I become more aware of God's presence all around me? Might I begin the practice of regular prayer sessions interspersed throughout my day? Perhaps reading a brief passage from the Bible and taking a few minutes to meditate on those words at various times during the day will help me to become more aware of God's presence in my life and his presence in the people and situations that fill my day. Might I consider taking a few minutes for silent prayer each day, praying without thoughts or words, aware only of God's presence surrounding me?

DAY TWELVE

Take Up Your Cross and Follow Me

FOCUS POINT

We are called to do God's will. There are many events and people that come into our lives unexpectedly, and we are oftentimes called to serve and give of ourselves even though it was not something we planned on doing. We bear many crosses as Christians, as God asks us to serve him in many different ways. We are called to respond to these crosses with joy, optimism, and love. As Christians, we are very much people of the present moment. What we've done before and what we plan on doing next weigh very little in comparison to what God calls us to do in the "now."

My Dear Bonetti,

When you receive this letter you will go find Don Rua and tell him, straight away, to make you happy. Don't speak about the breviary until Easter; that is, it is forbidden for you to recite it. Say your Mass slowly so it doesn't tire you. All fasts and mortifications concerning food are forbidden to you. In brief, the Lord is preparing you for work, but he doesn't want you to begin before you are in perfect health and rid of your cough. Do this and it will please the Lord.

You can compensate for those things through spontaneous prayer, through the offering of your worries to the Lord, and through your good example.

I was forgetting something. Put a mattress on your bed. Pamper yourself; cover yourself well, in and out of bed. Amen.

May God Bless you.

In the love of Jesus Christ,
Bosco Gio. Priest.
Turin, 1864.

LET US CARRY THE CROSS OF EACH DAY

Jesus' teaching is clear: "If any want to become my followers, let them deny themselves and take up their cross daily and follow me" (Lk 9:23).

John Bonetti, a young priest, had just joined his community in a new foundation in Piedmont. I had found him suffering. Upon returning to Turin, acting as a good "doctor" of both the soul and the body, I ordered him to get well! First, to avoid everything that could be the source of tension and fatigue: no breviary for four months, no fasting or deprivation with respect to food, and no haste in saying Mass—then, to compensate for these eases by short prayers, the offering of his worries, and the provision of a good example; without forgetting the precaution to sleep well and recover quickly! Finally, there is to be total abandonment to the Lord who loves his servant and counts on him for the harvest—and all of this in joy, confidence, and peace of heart. You are going to say to me: "But, Don Bosco, Jesus asks us to carry our cross daily and follow in his footsteps; where is the cross in your recommendations?" I would answer "that it's everywhere, but especially in a spirit of availability and service. Renunciation is not limited to mortifications and austerities. It is the equilibrium of life, self-control, concern for the health of the body in order to preserve that of the soul. It is a reply of love to the One who delivered himself for us on a cross; it is our commitment to follow him daily, patiently, courageously, as a faithful disciple who submits himself to a certain discipline. Like Jesus, we can say: "Father, if you are willing (as you wish)" (Lk 22:42). For me, this is the meaning of the daily cross that we must carry following Jesus.

CLOTHE THE NEW MAN

The apostle Paul declared: "...put away your former way of life, your old self...be renewed in the spirit of your minds... clothe yourselves with the new self..." (Eph 4:22–24). I experienced this transformation on two occasions at the beginning of my life.

When I took the habit, it was a kind of abandonment of "the old man." I was twenty and preparing to go into the seminary at Chieri. I felt the need to change my life. On October 25, 1835, in the parish church of Castelnuovo, my family and friends were in attendance. They knew me; they had applauded my exploits as an athlete, magician, musician, acrobat, hunter...what else? The ceremony began. The parish priest,

Don Cinzano, blessed the habit and presented it to me. Interiorly, I said this prayer: "Oh Lord, how many old habits must I get rid of! Make it so that I clothe myself with the new man and that I begin a new life, all according to your will." After that day, in order to give myself a rule for life, I wrote some resolutions. The first two noted a rupture and a radical choice: (1) in the future I will no longer attend any public spectacles at the fairs or at the marketplace; (2) I will no longer perform magic tricks; I will no longer play the violin; I will no longer go hunting. I find all of that to be contrary to the seriousness and the spirit of a cleric. Then, I made other resolutions regarding moderation in food and drink, vigilance over the heart and the senses, and prayer with a meditation and personal spiritual reading. I read these resolutions before a holy image of Mary, and decided to observe them at all cost. God alone had been witness to my faithfulness. This event freed me from my useless baggage, my old habits. In a way, it made me into a new man and committed me to the path of service.

Six years later, on June 5, 1841, in Turin, I was ordained a priest, an apostle completely dedicated to the mission of Christ. In order to be a "good soldier for Christ" it occurred to me that I had to become an ascetic. In my retreat notes, I read that the priest does not go to paradise alone. "If he acts well, he will go to heaven with the souls that he saved through his good example." My motto was already echoing in me: "Lord, give me the souls and take all of the rest." I wrote nine resolutions; the third and fourth being of central importance: "suffer, give oneself and humble oneself in everything and forever when we act to save souls"; and "may the charity and tenderness of Saint Francis de Sales guide me in all things." The other resolutions referred to temperance, amount of sleep (five hours a night), work, vigilance over the heart and the senses, and prayer— meditation, spiritual reading, and daily visits to the Blessed

Sacrament. One day, as a guide, I wrote, on a bookmark in my breviary, this thought of Saint Bernard: "Correct the sin you discover in yourself. Maintain what is right, repair what is broken, maintain what is beautiful, protect what is healthy, strengthen what is weak. Tirelessly read the Word of God; through it, you will sufficiently know the road to follow and the dangers to avoid." Thus, it seems to me that the new man developed within me.

LET US AWAIT OUR BLESSED HOPE

Christian asceticism is not sterile, it brings hope. The apostle Paul explained it to Titus, his friend: we must live "lives that are self-controlled, upright, and godly, while we wait for the blessed hope and the manifestation of the glory of our great God and savior, Jesus Christ" (Titus 2:12–13). Our hope is a person who gives meaning to the road of life. Listen to my ultimate message to three hundred Salesians gathered on a retreat; there you will find the essential elements of the spirituality of the cross that I tried to transmit to them. To each of them I had given a cross, and I said: "I recommend that you carry your cross, not the one of our choosing, but the one that is the will of God for us; and carry it gladly out of love. Let us then say: 'Oh blessed cross! Now you weigh nothing, but this will be of short duration. This cross will make us win a crown of roses for eternity....' Yes, my children, let us carry the cross with love, and not make it weigh on others. To the contrary, let us help others carry their crosses. Say to yourself: 'Certainly, I am a cross for others, just like others are often a cross for me; but I want to carry my cross without being one for others.' As well, tell yourself: 'This trial, this work, this illness, even though it seems light, also constitutes a cross. I carry each of them gladly and willingly because it is the cross the Lord has sent

me.' Always work for the glory of God...be happy, my dear
children, be healthy and holy, and always walk in agreement
among yourselves! Joy by the cross, and in the hope of living
with Jesus Christ forever!"

REFLECTION QUESTIONS

How do I respond to crosses that unexpectedly appear in my
life? Am I able to put aside what I had planned on doing in
favor of what God is calling me to do now? If I do struggle
with such unexpected crosses, might I consider bringing this to
my prayer life? Perhaps a style of prayer that helps me focus on
the present moment, removing my concentration from the past
and future, might benefit my spiritual life. Might I consult a
spiritual director as to what resources or methods of prayer
might be applicable?

DAY THIRTEEN

Choose a Guide for Your Journey

FOCUS POINT

As many times as we stumble in sin, God is there to pick us up and forgive us. His mercy is limitless, his love for us abiding. When we do sin and are forgiven by him, we must always recommit ourselves to the Lord, to following his Light, our Guide, Jesus Christ. And as we come to experience the forgiveness of God in our own lives, we are called to reflect this mercy in our own affairs. We have all been wronged by others, hurt sometimes by those people we trust so much. We can promote healing and love by our own willingness to forgive, sharing the merciful love we have known in our relationship with the Father.

Confession is a primary sign of God's mercy to sinners. If God had wanted to forgive our sins only through baptism, how many Christians would be lost! But knowing our great weakness, God wanted to institute another sacrament to redeem our sins committed after baptism. This sacrament is confession. (...) The confessor is a charitable father whose only goal is our salvation; he's a doctor who heals all of the scars in your soul (John Bosco, The Month of Mary, *Turin, 1858, days 21 and 22).*

"FATHER, I HAVE SINNED AGAINST HEAVEN AND BEFORE YOU" (LK 15:18)

The parable of the Prodigal Son brings to light God's tenderness. The father is God, who is rich in mercy. The father is the priest who offers forgiveness, a welcome, and gives confidence back to us, bringing peace to our hearts. I reminded my brother priests: "Whoever is a friend of the soul, inspires confidence. Confessors, with patience and gentleness, welcome all of your penitents, especially the children. Help them to open their conscience; insist that they come regularly to confession. Use all of your skills so that they put your advice into practice. Take them back with goodness, never scold them; for if you scold them, they will never come back nor will they ever truly be honest with you."

I reminded the young people that they should keep the same confessor. We don't change our friends like we change our clothing. "Faithful friends are a sturdy shelter: whoever finds one has found a treasure" (Sir 6:14).

"TAKE HEART, SON;
YOUR SINS ARE FORGIVEN" (MT 9:2)

When Jesus healed a paralyzed man who had been brought to him on a stretcher, he was impressed by the man's faith, and by the faith of those who carried him. He forgave that man's sins. He healed the heart before restoring health to the body—and what kindness is in his words: "Take heart, my son; your sins are forgiven"!

The confessor is a doctor who brings about healing. God's forgiveness transforms every recipient. But you're going to say to me: "Don Bosco, in ordinary time, what remedies do you propose to your penitents?" My orders—that is, the monitions—were short, simple, and practical, in line with the experiences and character of each person. One of my children preserved some of the words I had addressed to him in confession: "Think often of Jesus-Eucharist whose feast we celebrate today. Ask Mary to obtain for you, from her divine son, the grace of fervor. Dwell in peace…. Today, we begin the novena of the Immaculate Conception and are at the beginning of the school year. Put all of your heart into beginning this new year well, placing all of your actions under the protection of Mary. You will see how much she helps you! Go in peace."

I also invited my penitents to clearly mark their penance by a gesture. During the month of May, I proposed certain personal initiatives. For example: "I will forgive anyone who has hurt me; I will not let my eyes wander; I will not keep a certain object I hold dear; I will contemplate the cross of Jesus."

A true confession is evident through an amelioration of our life.

"STAND UP AND WALK" (MT 9:4)

Jesus forgave the sins of the paralyzed man, he restored health to his paralyzed body. "Get up, my friend, stand up and walk. Go home, you are a new man!" The crowd, amazed, gave thanks to God who had given such power to man. This power, Jesus himself transmitted to his brothers, to his priests. In his name, they can forgive; in his name, they can be spiritual guides. I myself have been guided and counseled throughout my life. Praise be the Lord for the counsels of my beloved mother Margaret. At the decisive stages of my childhood—first confession, first Communion—she said powerful words to me which affected my faith in God and my confidence in Mary. Praise the Lord for Don Calosso, the chaplain of my native hamlet. In his smile, in his goodness, and in his wisdom, it was your heart, Lord, I met. He counseled me about short daily meditation; thus I began to understand what a spiritual life was. Happy is the adolescent who finds a priest to open his heart and put him on the right path! Praise the Lord for the friend, the master, the holy priest Joseph Caffasso you placed on my path! Through him, the Holy Spirit counseled me, encouraged me, and guided me. In fact, he was my confessor and spiritual father for nineteen years. If I have done something good in my life, I owe it to this exceptional priest into whose hands I put all of my preoccupations and actions.

Praise the Lord for the youth and all people to whom I could give advice and comfort! Through the sacrament of forgiveness I verified the effectiveness of your grace in hearts. Praise the Lord for Savio, Magon, Besucco, and all the others! Their journey with us was too short.

Lord, you are truly the God of mercy. The grace of your forgiveness is a path of holiness, hope, and peace; it is a springtime for the heart. You are the God of love, always ready to tell us, once again: "Stand up and walk!"

REFLECTION QUESTIONS

How often do I participate in the sacrament of reconciliation? If this sacrament is not a regular part of my spiritual life, why is that? What is my experience of God's forgiving love? How does this experience of God's mercy carry over into my ability to forgive those people who have hurt me? Do I struggle with forgiveness, that is, the willingness to forgive others or even to forgive myself? If I do have a tendency to "hang on" to either wrongs done to me or sins I have committed (even after I have forgiven someone or have been forgiven myself), might I consider taking this concern to a spiritual director?

Receive the Bread of Each Day

FOCUS POINT

In the Eucharist, Jesus gives himself to us totally, to feed us, nourish us, and move us to love. This movement to love comes through service, a service Jesus displayed throughout the Gospel, throughout his life, culminating with the ultimate act of love, his sacrifice on the cross for our behalf. We are called to imitate Christ in the service of love, serving God by serving each other. We are called to be servants to one another, as Christ himself serves the people of God by giving himself to us daily in the Eucharist.

What tenderness there is in Jesus' love for man! In his infinite goodness, he established, with each of us, bonds of sublime love! He comes to dwell in our hearts with his body, soul, and divinity. What a marvelous gift! Jesus' love has no limits. With him, we form one single Body.

*Jesus could have limited his presence only to the celebration of Mass, but no! He wanted to make a permanent dwelling among us. Night and day he awaits us and offers himself to us at all times. Like a most tender mother, he opens his arms to us. He is there to generously give us his gifts. He is there to draw us to him and lead us to paradise with him. Oh! Let us go visit him often (*John Bosco, Novena in Honor of Mary, Help of Christians, *Turin, 1870, days 5 and 8).*

"WHOEVER EATS MY FLESH WILL LIVE THROUGH ME" (SEE JN 6:54–57)

The Eucharist is communion. One day, when I was in my second year at the seminary, I went to visit the Blessed Sacrament. Not having a book, I read a few chapters about the Eucharist, with interest, in *The Imitation of Christ.* This little golden book won me over and never left my side again. Could we not be inspired by it, by using the dialogic format between the Lord and his disciple? Let us begin this marvelous exchange.

The disciple: Jesus, I hear your voice whispering to me: "I am standing at the door and knocking." Yes, you call me by my name, by my first name, like Mary in the garden on Easter morning. Like Zacchaeus, I want to open my heart and my home. Come, I hunger for you. Sick, I await my Savior; poor, I receive my King; alone, I welcome my friend. Come, my door is open. Make yourself at home in my home!

Jesus Christ: If someone hears my voice, my son, and opens the door, I will enter his home. I will eat with him and he with me. Hear my voice! I am the bread of love, the bread that I give is the bread of my love. I loved all the way to this shared bread, and I loved you to the extreme. I had to travel a long road to come all the way to you. Faithful to my covenant, I fed the children of Israel in the desert with the manna of each day. I made myself flesh in Mary's womb, the tabernacle of beauty and purity. I multiplied the loaves of bread for the hungry crowd. But I had to love again. Before leaving my friends, I gathered them on the eve of my death and I told them: "My children, I will not leave you; take this bread, it is my body; drink from this cup, it is my blood. And do this gesture again, say my words again. In love, I remain with you until the end of time." Receive this bread of my love, my son, let your heart beat to the rhythm of my heart, and learn how to love. To love is to give, to share, and exchange. Be good bread for your brothers in the family, your place of work, your neighborhood—be nourishing bread. Whoever eats my flesh, lives through me, for my love is eternal. But also, my son, I am the living bread. In the desert, the bread gave strength and life to an entire people. On Easter morning, like a bud full of sap, I burst out of my tomb. The Holy Spirit awakened me from the dead and I was resurrected—I live forever. I am the living bread. My bread makes you live forever. It gives you my life like constantly renewed sap. It gives you my joy, the joy of the eternal Easter. Receive my life, you will live through me!

The disciple: My Lord and my God, I adore you in silence. Make it so that I, when my turn comes, will be the broken bread for my brothers, for a new world, for your glory, oh Jesus!

"SEE, THE HOME OF GOD IS AMONG MORTALS" (REV 21:3)

Jesus Christ: The Eucharist, my son, is also a place of adoration. After having spoken to my people in the burning bush, after having given them the bread of the desert, I pitched my tent among men. It is no longer the tent of the meeting with Moses, but the tabernacle of my real presence, of my permanent dwelling. I am the friend who stands watch, who welcomes, night and day, and who says: "Come to me, you who are overwhelmed with work and trials, I will soothe you."

The disciple: How marvelous your presence is, Lord! I adore you with the fervor of Dominic Savio, who spent hours in your company and spoke to you like a friend. A witness heard his words before the tabernacle: "Yes, my God, I say it to you, I say it to you again: I love you with all of my heart and I want to love you until I die." Is this not the sentiment of your presence that burst forth in John's cry on the edge of the water? "But yes, it's the Lord!" He's really there, it's him. One day, Dominic said: "The only thing that I'm missing to be happy on earth is to be able to rejoice in heaven, face to face, with the One I see in faith and whom I adore, today, on the altar." Willingly, he repeated this prayer in church: "Lord, I give you my freedom. Here are my strengths, here is my body, I give you everything—for everything is yours, my Lord. I abandon myself to your will, my God."

Jesus Christ: I made my dwelling close to you, my son, in the heart of your neighborhood, in your community. Do you understand that? Do you understand these last words to my apostles: "I am with you always, until the end of the world"? Every day I am near you, every day in the tabernacle my presence prolongs the eucharistic offering at the altar. Every day I repeat: "I will arise from the earth, I will draw everyone to me." Today I draw you to me, my son. Would you offer yourself with me?

The disciple: Yes Lord. I dedicate myself completely to you, on the cross and in the tabernacle. Come fill me up again with your love. Jesus, take my eyes, my wounding glances, and my egoistic blindness; give me your eyes, so I may be marveled at myself as you are and so I can see with your heart. Jesus, take my hands which are so often lazy; give me your hands, so I may share and serve, work and build; your hands that were pierced with nails so I may offer myself to your Father with you! Jesus, take my gluttonous and lying lips, give me your own lips so I may be silent and pray, bless and give thanks, smile and sing. Jesus, take my heart with its harshness and anger, and give me your heart; a peaceful heart to make peace, a heart to give without concern, a humble and gentle heart so I can recognize you in the person who is the most impoverished. You are there, Lord; I give myself to you and I adore you, by saying the words of the *Adoro Te*: "Oh memorial of the death of the Lord, living bread who gives life to man, grant my soul to live with you and to always experience the gentleness of your presence."

"I HAVE SET YOU AN EXAMPLE" (JN 13:15)

Jesus Christ: Adoration, my son, leads to imitation. Imitation transforms and commits. Have you meditated on the gesture that I made at the Last Supper with my friends? I tied a cloth to my belt and washed the feet of my disciples; and I wiped them. The meal continued. I said: "I have given you the example so that you will also be able to do what I have done for you." Then I shared the bread, showing, from this time on, that the breaking of the bread is connected to service, the eucharistic liturgy is linked to the liturgy of life. The person who takes Communion will make himself a servant like me!

The disciple: The words of the beloved apostle remain in my heart: "Jesus gave his life for us; when it is our turn, we must give our lives for our brothers." The first Christians experienced this; they were diligent in the breaking of the bread and they shared their goods, and manifested their faith through gestures of friendship and reconciliation. But today, Lord, how do we interpret the gestures that accompanied the first Eucharist? How do we live the example that you gave us?

Jesus Christ: I gave you the example, my son, first, in order to remind man that the first quality of service is that it's freely given. Contemporary society has multiplied services and functions of all kinds. Service has often become synonymous with strength, power, and money.

According to the Gospel, the servant is disinterested. The one who has received a great deal should share, the one who governs should be the one who serves. Be disinterested servants. I gave you the example so that "you will wash each other's feet" in all humility. According to the Gospel, the servant is humble. Humility does not consist of being small or poor, but in making oneself small and poor at heart, in lowering oneself and becoming "condescendent" through love. The greater the one who loves is, the more he makes himself humble all the way to the total gift of himself, all the way to the cross. We spoke of the "humility of God." The servant hears my call: "Learn that I am gentle and humble of heart." Service is the source of all virtues. After having loved my loved ones, I loved them all the way to the end, all the way to washing their feet, then to sharing bread with them. I gave them the example so that my service would prove my love through the strength of the Holy Spirit. Through service, we see the beginning of the kingdom of heaven.

The disciple: Lord, in faith, I adore you. In the Eucharist, as in the Incarnation, you reveal yourself to me. I repeat the words of the hymn: "Jesus, up until now, when I contemplated you, your face was veiled, I beg you to make it so that I realize my ardent desire to see you, face to face, unveiled, and establish my happiness in the vision of your glory!"

REFLECTION QUESTIONS

Is the Eucharist an important part of my spiritual life? Do I see the relationship between the Eucharist and my call to serve? In what ways does the Eucharist motivate me to imitate Christ? How does my consumption of the Eucharist at Mass transform me and motivate my desire to serve outside of church? Is it difficult for me at times to live as a servant? Do I find it a struggle to humble myself in certain situations, with specific people? Might I consider reading the Gospels on a regular basis to aid my desire for humility, and live in service and imitation of the Servant who never fails to love me?

DAY FIFTEEN
I Wait for All of You in Paradise

FOCUS POINT

Don Bosco's love and concern for the welfare of the people of God (particularly children) is undeniable. The idea of a strong community, a family united in love, in God, permeates the spirituality of Don Bosco. He champions the wonderful acts of love we can provide for one another—acts of love that spring forth from knowing the love and mercy God has for each of us and imitating the love shown by Jesus that we read about in the Gospels. United in love for God and one another, Don Bosco recognizes the great support we give each other in following God's call and doing his will as we journey to be united with the Father in eternity.

My dear and much beloved sons in Jesus Christ, I leave you on this earth, but only for a short time. I hope that the infinite mercy of God allows us to, one day, find ourselves in blessed eternity. It is there that I await you. Continue to love me through the exact observance of our constitutions. Your first superior is dead. But your true superior, Jesus Christ, doesn't die. He will always be our master, our guide, our model. So long, oh my dear children, so long! I await you in heaven! There, we will speak about God, about Mary, the mother and support of our congregation; there, we will eternally bless this congregation in which obedience to the rules would have strongly and effectively contributed to saving us (John Bosco, Spiritual Testament, *Turin, 1884).*

"HE WILL BRING US WITH YOU INTO HIS PRESENCE"

At the beginning of these meditations, I proclaimed, for you my friends, the beatitudes as a road to happiness. Blessed are you if you live these paths of freedom and joy daily. The kingdom is within you; I promised you it would burst, one day, into the eternal springtime of paradise. That is possible, for "the one who raised the Lord Jesus will raise us also with Jesus, and will bring us with you into his presence" (2 Cor 4:14). Thus, the Holy Spirit who raised Jesus from the dead, will raise us on the last day and place us into his presence forever—such is the happiness and joy without end in paradise. There, I will find myself next to the living God; there, I will await you. For, where I am, you will also be; your place is reserved. I remind you: the secret of your happiness is the success of your life, your vocation, no matter what your age or condition. Walk in hope, with your eyes towards the homeland!

I await you, parents and teachers. Today, like before, your duty is a "ministry," an irreplaceable profession in the eyes of both God and society. It is a battle for dignity, justice, and the success of both the Christian and the citizen, a battle against rejections and excesses of all kinds. Education is an affair of the heart. Love your children and your students more than yourself; they were created in the image and likeness of God, they are tenderly loved by the Father, saved in Jesus Christ. The Holy Spirit dwells in them to guide them, and strengthen them in virtue. It is the teacher, the amazing counselor who inspires and calms them. Love the young people with the heart of God, with his patience, his tenderness, his humility, his gentleness. My entire method is based on the Gospel. Like Jesus, let us know how to forgive, reconcile, assemble, trust, and sow joy that lasts. Like him, may we repeat: "Get up and walk!" Love the young people, not as inferiors, but like people full of promise. The teacher is not someone who knows, but someone who humbly makes his way on the road of progress, of holiness. Love what the young people love, but also admit that they like other things than we do. For education, just like the love of a couple, promotes differences, goes through denial, and builds itself up through failures and successes. Love the young people and, with special concern, the poorest, those who are excluded, those who have been broken down through failures, those who escape through drug use, often because they have been poorly loved or rejected. The Lord's warning is serious: I am the poor, the little ones! Yes, my friends, education is a privileged place for a personal meeting with the risen Jesus: "whoever welcomes one such child in my name welcomes me" (Mt 18:5). Education is also an affair of reason, dialogue, and of the formation of judgment. We must remember this in this century of images. Let us have confidence. Often, I repeated the following: "Without affection, there is no trust; without

trust, there is no education." Today, children are often too protected; effort is avoided; everything is given to them, without
any effort or initiative of their own. Give them a sense of responsibility. I taught young people to commit themselves in
service to their brothers, to cooperate with God; I trained them
to become apostles. Happiness, just like true love, requires us
to go to other people. That is your responsibility, parents and
teachers. Be strong! Education, a path towards God, leads to
paradise! I await all of you there. And you, who are participat-
ing in these "fifteen days of prayer with Don Bosco," may the
same hope inspire you: "The glory of God is the living man,
man's life is God's vision" (Saint Irenaeus).

"LET US GO TO THE HOUSE OF THE LORD!"

The words of this "psalm of ascent" towards the shrine of
Jerusalem gives life to our progression to paradise. There I
wait for you, friends, priests, religious, and lay people committed to the Church in service to its mission. You are all God's
collaborators, you are all responsible in your diocesan com-
munities, parishes, and movements. Be faithful and disinterested servants, artisans of peace and unity, joyous in your faith,
following the example of the first Christians. I, myself, a priest
in the diocese of Turin, a religious involved with lay people,
repeated this insistently during my lifetime. Remember Jesus
Christ who rose from the dead; may he remain your master,
your guide, your model. Just as Saint Paul said to Timothy, I
said to my fellow priests: "rekindle the gift of God that is within
you through the laying on of my hands" (2 Tim 1:6); that is
the grace of your ordination, to choose God and love him more
than anything each day. Share the bread of the Eucharist which
is the Church, and invite others to do the same; live God's
forgiveness, the springtime of God and renewal of love. Be pas-

sionate about the Gospel, proclaim it to the youth and especially to the most underprivileged, to the marginalized, to those who are handicapped in their bodies and their hearts; be witnesses of God for them; through your smile and your joy you will awaken vocations as apostles and as saints. Religious brothers and sisters, keep the spirit of your congregations like a precious treasure, remain faithful to your holy vows—we don't take back what has been given to God. Everyone, be loving children to the Church our mother, carriers of the wealth of Vatican II, and open to the renewal of prayer, liturgy, the humanities, and theology. Dwell under the gaze and the mantle of Mary, our most gentle and good mother, remain confident of her help and you will see miracles. Awaken Christians from their "sleep" in order to await the return of the Lord. Revive familiarity, nostalgia, and the meaning of the celestial homeland to the faithful. The world beyond is not an alienation, but an Easter, a passage to the Light. The world beyond is "the blessed hope and the manifestation of the glory of our great God and Savior, Jesus Christ" (Titus 2:13). Follow the road to happiness. I await you in the peace of God!

"SING PRAISE TO HIM AND HIGHLY EXALT HIM FOREVER" (AZAR/SONG THR 1:35)

Finally, I await you, young people of all countries, of all races, "the delights of God's heart." You are the builders of this world in the twenty-first century. Through your actions, communicate your joy in believing in the living Christ!

Yes! I promised God that my life, right to my very last breath, would be dedicated to young people. I believe I have kept my word. I loved you, and I tried to make you feel it. I always tried to understand and love what you loved. To all the young people and their teachers I said: "Confidence and friendship must be established relentlessly between you. Be agents of union and not separation. You can do nothing alone."

I always wanted your happiness; always be happy and seek peace in your hearts daily. This joy and this peace will go beyond the borders. Run, jump, shout, sing, make music. Be completely free; live as sons and daughters of God, and may Mary, our helper, always help you to faithfully keep the love of Jesus who has always been the very heart of my life.

My friends, I await all of you in paradise! I tell you, as I did at the altar: "Lift up your hearts! Our God is the God of all joy! Glory and power to him" (see Rev 19). Hallelujah!

Before leaving, I invite you to pray with me:

Holy Spirit, give us a universal heart
so we can remain attentive,
each day, to all calls of distress.
Give us clear vision,
peace in our smile, to reveal to man
the star he carries in his heart.
Give us an unending zeal
to make our lives a response of love
in service to the most underprivileged.
Under the gaze of Mary, our most gentle mother,
make us faithful servants for the harvest,
pilgrims of hope on the road to paradise.
Amen.

REFLECTION QUESTIONS

What is my understanding of the spirituality of Saint John Bosco as I conclude these fifteen days of prayer? What one or two aspects of this spirituality would I like to foster in my own life? Considering Don Bosco's great love for and commitment to community, how has my own perception of what community (parish community, family community) should be evolving? How can I help to bring this ideal of community to life in my own parish, in my own family? What role might regular participation in the sacraments play in my spiritual development?

Bibliography

Beebe, Catherine. *Saint John Bosco and Saint Dominic Savio*. Ignatius Press, 1992.

Bosco, John. *Memoirs of the Oratory of Saint Francis de Sales From 1815 to 1855: The Autobiography of Saint John Bosco*. Translated by Daniel Lyons. Salesiana Publications, 1990.

Brown, Eugene, ed. *Dreams, Visions & Prophecies of Don Bosco*. Don Bosco Publications, 1986.

Desramaut, Francis. *Don Bosco and the Spiritual Life*. Translated by Roger M. Luna. Salesiana Publications, 1979.

Lappin, Peter. *Give Me Souls! Life of Don Bosco*. Salesiana Publications, 1986.

Morrison, John A. *The Educational Philosophy of Saint John Bosco*. Salesiana Publications, 1997.

Rinaldi, Peter M. *Man With a Dream: The Story of Saint John Bosco*. Salesiana Publications, 1978.

Stella, Pietro. *Don Bosco: Life and Work*. Translated by John Drury. Salesiana Publications, 1996.

———. *Don Bosco: Religious Outlook and Spirituality*. Translated by John Drury. Salesiana Publications, 1996.

Wirth, Morand. *Don Bosco and the Salesians*. Translated by David DeBurgh. Salesiana Publications, 1982.